Experimental
Syntax

Experimental
Syntax

Applying Objective Methods
to Sentence Judgments

Wayne Cowart

SAGE Publications
International Educational and Professional Publisher
Thousand Oaks   London   New Delhi

For information address:

 SAGE Publications, Inc.
2455 Teller Road
Thousand Oaks, California 91320
E-mail: order@sagepub.com

SAGE Publications Ltd
1 Oliver's Yard
55 City Road
London EC1Y 1SP

SAGE Publications India Pvt Ltd
B-42, Panchsheel Enclave
Post Box 4109
New Delhi 110 017

Printed in the United States of America

Library of Congress Cataloging-in-Publication Data

Cowart, Wayne.
    Experimental syntax: Applying objective methods to sentence
judgments / author, Wayne Cowart.
      p.   cm.
    Includes bibliographical references and index.
    ISBN 0-7619-0042-X (alk. paper).—ISBN 0-7619-0043-8 (pbk.:
alk. paper)
      1. Grammar, Comparative and general—Syntax. 2. Linguistics—
Methodology. 3. Acceptability (Linguistics) I. Title.
    P291.C68 1996
    415—dc20   96-35620

97 98 99 00 01 02 03 10 9 8 7 6 5 4 3 2 1

Acquiring Editor:	Alex Schwartz
Editorial Assistant:	Eileen Carr
Production Editor:	Diana E. Axelsen
Production Assistant:	Denise Santoyo
Typesetter & Designer:	Andrea D. Swanson
Indexer:	Virgil Diodato
Cover Designer:	Ravi Balasuriya

Contents

Preface

This book provides an introduction to objective methods by which linguists and others may describe patterns of sentence acceptability in speech communities. An investigator with a well-formed question about a matter of fact relative to sentence acceptability is shown how to design, execute, and analyze an appropriate experiment. The book is augmented by software tools relevant to various aspects of the preparation, execution, and analysis of survey experiments, plus a number of example files. These materials are provided by way of the World Wide Web site maintained by the Linguistics Program at the University of Southern Maine, at http:/www.usm.maine.edu/~lin.

The book is intended primarily for those whose background in syntactic theory is more extensive than their background in experimentation and statistical analysis. It should be useful to a range of people from seasoned syntactic researchers who have not previously used experimental methods to students who are new to both syntactic research and experimental methods. Those who come to the book with a strong background in experimental work will find many passages can be skimmed without loss. Although the book will discuss a variety of statistical issues, it is not intended to be a text in statistics or general research design. Rather, the aim is to show how mostly commonplace principles of these disciplines can be brought to bear on experiments on sentence judgments. The text will point out some statistical topics and sources along the way but will discuss statistical issues only insofar as necessary to specify and justify appropriate methods for experiments on sentence judgments.

The main thread of the discussion will present all the theoretical and practical issues an investigator needs to be aware of to design and execute meaningful experiments on judgments of acceptability. Two kinds of supplementary material appear in appendixes at the back of the book. First, although Chapter 1 reports on a number of experimental findings, the chapter is meant to be approachable for readers with no prior background in statistics. Thus only informal accounts of the results appear in the main text of Chapter 1. More detailed statistical reporting on the results presented in this chapter appears in Appendix B. Second, the main discussion in the book will not deal with software tools and techniques relevant to executing the methods described. Some readers familiar with word processing and spreadsheet software will be able to work their way through the process on their own. Those who want more specific guidance on how to use software tools to carry out the various tasks that constitute the preparation, execution, and analysis of an experiment will find relevant discussion in Appendix C.

The term *objective methods* in the title of the book perhaps deserves brief comment. Sentence judgments appear to arise within human subjective experience. Although there seems to be a threat of controversy at every turn in the discussion of consciousness, I will assume the classical view that consciousness is a domain of private experience closed to all external observers. How then can there be objective methods for the study of a subjective phenomenon? Philosophers of science noticed some time back that so-called objective observations were themselves subjective experiences, not fundamentally different than any other sort of subjective experience.[1] Rather, what distinguishes those experiences we call objective observations from others is that they are those on which we can achieve intersubjective agreement. In other terms, these are the observations where different observers can reliably agree on what counts as an appropriate linguistic expression of the observation (e.g., "The meter is reading 3.7." "The reddish-brown layer is below the whitish one." "This patient is aphasic."). From this vantage point, it requires only a relatively small step to get to a notion of "objectivity" relevant to the study of sentence judgments.

Although the immediate evanescent experience of a sentence, including the sense that it is, or is not, acceptable, seems to be inescapably private, the communicative integrity of linguistic communities rests, by hypothesis, on shared grammars. That is, we expect that different members of a given linguistic community will be led to similar experiences of a very wide range of sentences by a grammar that they hold, more or less, in common. In terms of Chomsky's notion of I-language (Chomsky, 1986), being a functioning member of a linguistic community depends upon achieving some degree of (rather intricate) alignment between one's own unique, private, I-language and the typical or normal patterns of the I-languages of other members of one's community. Indeed, each speaker's I-language can be seen as an estimate of the grammatical norms of the community (or communities) within which the individual acquired language and currently uses it, although this estimate is obviously subject to distortion by a variety of factors operating on the acquisition process and the generally slower and perhaps less orderly processes of grammatical change in adults.

Thus there is an object of linguistic inquiry that becomes approachable via intersubjective methods. This is the standard or average pattern of judgments across sets of related sentences within a coherent linguistic community. By asking for judgments from many individuals, we can uncover typical patterns of judgments within communities; these patterns should bear on theories of the grammars that shape those judgments. Variants of these methods may also be useful in providing reliable descriptions of the patterns of response typical of individual speakers, but as we'll see in Chapter 2, the problem of reliably characterizing individuals is far harder than detecting differences in judgments across sentence types.

The leap from objective observations of the external world to intersubjective observations of the inner world is not so great as it first appears. In the classical objective case, we assume that there is some external reality that governs and constrains, and thus accounts for, the commonalities in the reported subjective experiences (i.e., the observations) of different observers. When we apply intersubjective methods to the study of human grammars, we assume that there is some inner reality in the brains of the speakers we test that governs and constrains, and thus accounts for, the commonalities and structure in the reported experiences of each individual speaker, and also that similarities across speakers are explained by similarities in this inner reality.

Acknowledgments

    The project out of which this work arises has been in development for some time and has benefited from comments and suggestions from many sources. My greatest debt is to my colleague Dana McDaniel, who has collaborated extensively on some of the experimental work reported here and has contributed in innumerable ways to the project as a whole. Helen Cairns has commented ever so faithfully and usefully on many drafts of papers and chapters related to this work. I am also indebted to her for passing along to me a certain "picky-picky" tradition in the construction of example sentences that arose at the University of Texas in the 1960s. I hope this work will contribute something to that tradition by helping to better describe differences among sentences of the "same" type. Jennifer Hsu, Fritz Newmeyer, Ken Pugh, and Nancy Richards also read and commented on all or part of the manuscript, each providing very helpful suggestions. Tom Bever was instrumental in sparking a certain biological turn in my thinking that led to heightened interest in syntactic patterns in populations and the individual members of those populations. Michael Studdert-Kennedy fostered my interest in biological perspectives on language before I could figure out quite how or whether I wanted to address such issues. Diana Smetters and Ken Williams helped to get this line of research going by running two of the earlier experiments reported here.

I am very grateful to Carson Schütze for providing a draft of his recent volume (1996) on grammaticality judgments. His thoroughgoing and scholarly review of the literature in this area has been an invaluable aid.

Ed Battistella at Wayne State College and David Basilico at the University of Alabama at Birmingham provided indispensable assistance in collecting data on their campuses. Although almost none of the data are used here, I am also very grateful to colleagues at the University of Arizona and Queens College/CUNY for extraordinary cooperation with a recent large experiment (as yet unpublished) that contributed significantly to the project out of which this book has grown. At Arizona, Rudy Troike and Tom Miller, as well as many of their colleagues in the Composition Program, helped us collect hundreds of responses from undergraduates there. At Queens College, Helen Cairns and several instructors in the Linguistics Program helped us collect many responses there as well.

Len Katz provided some helpful suggestions on statistical issues. Guy Carden and Hiroshi Nagata provided copies of papers that proved quite useful at various stages of this project.

I also benefited from comments and questions from members of the audience at presentations and colloquia on parts of this work at CLS '89, ESCOL '90, LSA '90, LSA '96, University of Massachu-setts/Amherst, Haskins Laboratories, City University of New York, and the University of New Hampshire.

Although I have benefited from the assistance, advice, and/or cooperation of all of these colleagues, they bear no responsibility for such foolishness as may remain in this text. All defects in the book are solely due to the tiny green bugs that seemed to rain down on the manuscript whenever I worked on it in my backyard.

The experimental work reported here was supported in part by grants from the National Science Foundation, SBR-9422688 (awarded to the author and Dana McDaniel), and the National Institutes of Health, R01 NS22606.

Finally, and mostly, I am grateful to Judy and Cayce for repay-ing my neglect with much more patience and affection than I think I'm entitled to.

Note

1. See Popper (1959/1935, pp. 44-48) for some comments on the role of inter-subjective agreement in establishing scientific observations.

Web Site for This Book

Some Excel spreadsheets and other tutorial materials relevant to the topics this book discusses are available at the following site on the World Wide Web:

http:/www.usm.maine.edu/~lin

1

Introduction: Are Judgments Stable?

So far as research practice is concerned, one of the most striking contrasts between generative linguistics and its immediate predecessors lies in the fundamental importance assigned to speakers' introspective judgments of sentence acceptability (Chomsky, 1957, 1986). In an earlier era, Bloomfield (1930) had specifically rejected reference to the speaker's internal states as beyond the reach of science. Chomsky instead embraced introspective judgments as an essential tool for the exploration of the mental resources underlying language use. This move has been extremely fruitful. The new data made available to linguists via the inclusion of judgments of sentence acceptability have, in conjunction with other innovations, brought a vast array of syntactic phenomena within the reach of contemporary theory. Whatever the merits of various theoretical enterprises, there is no doubt that we now have access to an enormous treasure of descriptive generalizations about sentence structure in a wide range of languages

1

that could never have been acquired without reliance on judgment data.

Nevertheless, there have been continuing doubts about the empirical reliability and theoretical interpretation of judgment data as well as questions about what constitutes an appropriate technique for gathering judgment data. A variety of authors have alleged that judgments are gravely compromised by instability of several different kinds. Some have found evidence of extreme disagreements from informant to informant (or linguist to linguist) while others have reported evidence that informants often disagree with themselves if responses given on different occasions are compared. Others have suggested that the orderly and consistent patterning of judgments across various theoretically related sentence types occurs, if at all, in the judgments of linguists, but not in the unstudied responses of typical speakers. These uncertainties are complicated by the fact that there seems to be no consensus on how to gather judgments apart from a widespread tolerance of informal methods in which the linguist consults her own intuitions and those of the first handy informant (what we might call the "Hey, Sally" Method). Further, the lack of any consensus on just how judgments are related to grammars (what, if anything, is the difference between grammaticality and acceptability) has sometimes been seen as an insuperable bar to any scientifically appropriate use of judgments.

This book has a simple purpose that bears on these issues; it will describe a family of practical methods that yield demonstrably reliable data on patterns of sentence acceptability in populations of linguistically naive speakers. This chapter will review some evidence that the methods to be described here do in fact yield reliable results. However, the bulk of the book is a tutorial intended to allow a researcher with little or no prior training in experimental work to design and execute small-scale experiments that yield reliable data on the kinds of judgment issues syntacticians typically care about. Thus, for the most part, the book ignores prior debates about the stability and interpretation of judgment data, focusing instead on describing a sound practical technique whose merits can be independently assessed by interested investigators. The book will not be much concerned with some notions related to stability in the psychology and statistics literatures.[1] The best source a reader may turn to for a general review of the history and theory of judgments in linguistics is Carson Schütze's volume, *The Empirical Base of Linguistics* (1996).

Before launching into a practical explication of the method, there are some background issues that need to be addressed. First, the next section will briefly review some of the kinds of evidence that have raised doubts about the stability of judgment data, as well as some potentially relevant data from allied disciplines that suggest that the problems of stability may not be as bad as is sometimes alleged. Second, we will ask whether there is any way that grammatical theory can or should constrain our approach to measuring acceptability—especially where a grammatical theory posits only two (or a very few) degrees of grammaticality. This section also asks what it means to claim that a particular kind of data is or is not stable.

In the third and fourth parts of this introductory chapter, we turn to empirical evidence that stable patterns of judgments occur among linguistically naive informants. This section lays out a number of experimental findings that come from applications of the methods described in the rest of the book. These results will demonstrate that the methods do in fact produce reliable data of the kind that bear on syntactic theory.

The chapter ends with an overview of the rest of the book.

1.1 Doubts About the Stability of Judgments

Linguists were not the first to use introspective judgments in a scientific context. Introspective judgments of various kinds were widely applied in psychological investigations in the late nineteenth and early twentieth centuries. During this era, psychologists studied a variety of conscious phenomena via introspective methods. Yet, despite their wide application and acceptance, many varieties of introspective procedures were generally rejected earlier in this century in part because of evidence that the results of these procedures were unstable, seeming to vary across individuals and laboratories. Boring's (1953) historical review of introspection suggests, however, that the rejection of introspection was more theoretical than practical. Many of the conscious phenomena that had been the focus of introspective investigation continued to be studied, often by quite similar means. Verbal reports that were once interpreted as evidence of private conscious states now became objects of study in themselves; instead of asking why consciousness took such and such a form, the psychologist asked instead why the verbal report took such and such a form. What changed in the behaviorist era had to do more with the theory of what consciousness is (or isn't) than with a thoroughgoing rejection of introspective method.

Doubts about the stability of judgment data began to appear in the linguistic literature very soon after the emergence of generative linguistics. As early as 1961, Hill reported on a very informal study of several nonnaive informants in which he found substantial disagreement about the status of several of the 10 sentences he examined (Hill, 1961). In the early 1970s, Carden (1970, 1973) found evidence of dialect differences among naive informants as to how negatives and quantifiers interact in certain circumstances. Other participants in the subsequent discussion (Heringer, 1970; Labov, 1972; Stokes, 1974, among others) also found evidence of substantial disagreements among informants.[2] Labov (1975) called attention to differences in experimentally derived judgments reported in these and related papers. Snow and Meijer (1977) collected judgment data from Dutch informants on 24 sentences via both a rating and a ranking procedure. Although they found substantial agreement among informants on sentence rankings, there was no significant correlation between the ratings and rankings obtained from individual informants (provided at separate sessions 1 week apart). Snow and Meijer were primarily impressed by the evidence of instability they found.

Ross (1979) describes a study in which 30 informants, including some linguists, were asked to rate 13 sentences in various ways. Although Ross is quite candid about the statistical limitations of his analysis (the work being intended essentially as a pilot study), he finds much evidence of disagreement among informants about the status of particular sentences. He found subsets of informants that agreed on a few sentences, but no two informants provided the same ratings for even a third of the sentences. Ross also noted that informants seemed to be least likely to agree on more peripheral items that show generally low acceptability.

A very thorough and careful critique of judgment data appears in Labov (1975). In a review of numerous published and unpublished findings, Labov found extensive evidence of disagreements among informants. He also found many disagreements between published assessments of sentences in the linguistics literature and the assessments of naive informants. He concluded that variation in judgments was widespread and disorderly enough to call into question much work based on intuitive data.

A number of investigators have found evidence that individual informants can give different assessments on different occasions or under different conditions (Carroll, Bever, & Pollack, 1981; Nagata, 1987a, 1987b, 1988, 1989a, 1989b, 1989c, 1989d, 1992; Snow & Meijer, 1977). Labov (1975) also concludes that informant judgments don't always agree with the informant's own linguistic behavior, raising questions about both the stability and the interpretation of those judgments.

There is also considerable anecdotal evidence of variability in judgments from linguists who teach syntactic theory. In both graduate and undergraduate courses, it seems to be commonplace for students to disagree with judgments given in texts and the research literature. Although these disagreements may sometimes reflect misunderstanding of the issues relevant to a given sentence, such disagreements are too commonplace to be dismissed lightly.

Despite these indications of significant instability in judgment data, there is also evidence that sentence judgments are, at least some of the time, highly stable. Some debates in syntactic theory turn on relatively small differences in judged acceptability, but there remain many contrasts that are quite dramatic. If, for example, one is concerned with the standard ordering of the major elements of the English clause, there will be little or no variation in relevant judgments. Personal introspection may be reliable for some of these syntactic contrasts. Newmeyer (1983) also argues that many disagreements over judgments are only apparent, and that, whatever the limitations of judgment data, their manifest utility in furthering syntactic research far outweighs whatever limitations attach to them.

Given the skepticism described above, it is perhaps surprising that judgments of "grammaticality" have found increasing use in the psychological literature. Roughly 60 papers over the last two decades have used one or another grammaticality judgment method, about 40 of these in the last decade. Many of these papers report some variety of judgment procedure that is potentially relevant to linguistic issues. In addition to issues in general cognitive psychology and language processing (e.g., Ferreira & Henderson, 1991), these papers have addressed questions in neurolinguistics (e.g., Berndt, Salasoo, Mitchum, & Blumstein, 1988; Blumstein, Milberg, Dworetzky, Rosen, & Gershberg, 1991; Linebarger, Schwartz, & Saffran, 1983; Wulfeck & Bates, 1991), L1 and L2 acquisition (e.g., Ellis, 1991; Schachter & Yip, 1990), reading (e.g., Fowler, 1988), and the cognitive theory of judgment process (e.g., Carroll et al., 1981; Cowart, 1994; Gerken & Bever, 1986; Nagata, 1987a, 1987b, 1988, 1989a, 1989b, 1989c, 1989d, 1990, 1991, 1992).[3]

There is a notable contrast between most psychological uses of judgments and a number of the linguistic studies that have criticized judgments on the basis of experimental findings. Many of the experimental linguistic studies mentioned above tacitly assume that each encounter between an informant and a sentence yields (at least in the great majority of cases) a definitive index of that informant's assessment of that sentence. In statistical terms, these studies assume that there is little or no "error variance" in sentence judgments (the concept of error variance will be discussed in the next chapter). Surprisingly few linguistic attempts to study judgments experimentally have given serious consideration to the possibility that an informant's judgments might be subject to some amount of random variation around a stable mean. Another important feature of some of the linguistic studies mentioned above is that they effectively assume that each sentence is a definitive representative of its syntactic type, sometimes using only a single representative of each sentence type tested. Such practices make no allowance for the widely recognized fact that lexical differences between different tokens of the same syntactic type can produce quite substantial differences in judged acceptability. Many of these studies also ascribe no significance to order, in effect assuming that the order in which a set of sentences is presented exerts no effect on judged acceptability.

The contrast to standard practice in psychophysics is particularly striking. Like much of contemporary syntactic research, psychophysics is very much concerned with descriptions of the private subjective states of human subjects. In the case of psychophysics, however, the private states in question are generally responses to relatively simple external physical events such as flashes of light, brief tones, touches of the subject's skin, and so on. Even with these far simpler stimuli, it is commonplace to have each subject judge dozens or even hundreds of instances of *the same stimulus*. This effort is undertaken for the simple reason that subjects routinely give variable responses to different presentations of a single stimulus. By asking each subject to judge each stimulus many times, psychophysicists are able to establish highly reliable descriptions of those responses that will generalize to future sessions with the same subject and to data collected from other subjects as well. From a linguistic point of view, this bears emphasis: Although there are many stimuli for which each subject's responses will show a highly stable norm, it is often difficult to detect that norm on the basis of small numbers of responses. The nature of sentences obviously makes it inappropriate to present the same sentence to one informant many times,[4] but there may be an important hint in standard psychophysical practice and experience that the normal variability of individual sentence judgments could be much higher than linguists have generally assumed. The next chapter will pursue this issue in more detail.

1.2 Grammatical Theory and the Measurement of Acceptability

Part of the task of devising and justifying sound objective methods for gathering judgment data—methods that can put to rest the doubts and concerns raised above—is to adopt a clear and defensible view of the relation between grammatical theory and the process of forming judgments. I will assume that theories of grammar are partial models of the human cognitive system that should, among other things, help to explain why judgments pattern as they do. The principal question here is whether there is any aspect of grammatical theory that can or should constrain the procedures by which judgment data are gathered or analyzed. In particular, because grammatical theories sometimes countenance only a few different degrees of grammaticality, is there any way that this feature ought to affect the collection or analysis of judgment data?

Chomsky (1965) provides a relatively straightforward answer to this question in what has become the classical position on the role of judgments of sentence acceptability in generative theory. In this view,[5] which exploits the distinction between competence and performance, the act of forming or expressing a judgment of acceptability is a kind of linguistic performance. The grammar that a linguistic theory posits in the head of a speaker does not exercise exhaustive control of judgments any more than it exercises exhaustive control of the processes of uttering or comprehending sentences. While forming a sentence judgment, a speaker draws on a variety of cognitive resources to perceive the auditory or visual signals through which the sentence is expressed, to parse or process the sentence as its elements are identified, to form an evaluation of the sentence, and to organize and execute a response. Among the cognitive resources the speaker will draw on in executing a performance of this kind there is, by hypothesis, a grammar. Even if every component works optimally, whatever influence the grammar achieves arises in collaboration, or perhaps competition, with other components of the cognitive system. Whatever pattern of grammaticality values a grammar might assign to a set of sentences, the grammar relies on the rest of the cognitive system to instantiate those grammaticality values in overt judgments of acceptability. The resulting judgments could pattern quite differently than the grammaticality values we might like them to reflect.

Needless to say, with these assumptions, however many degrees of grammaticality the grammar might distinguish, the grammar's interactions with other components could easily yield judgments that are more (or less) finely differentiated than the grammaticality values the grammar provides.[6]

Within this frame of reference, judgments of acceptability provide evidence that bears on theories of grammar, but that evidence is not always subject to easy interpretation. As Bever (1974) noted, this model of acceptability judgments implies that the study of judgments and their implications for the theory of grammar will proceed in parallel with the study of the full network of cognitive resources involved in executing judgments. Patterns of results that emerge in judgment data are potentially explained by reference to (a) a model of grammar, (b) other components of the cognitive system, or (c) interactions between the grammar and those other components. For example, it is widely accepted that extragrammatical components or features of the processing system (e.g., memory limitations) can make fully grammatical sentences difficult in ways that show up as low acceptability ratings, and it is at least conceivable that extragrammatical components of the system could "rescue" ungrammatical sentences, giving them higher acceptability ratings than their grammatical status would predict (see Langendoen & Bever, 1973, and Bever, 1974, for suggestions as to how this situation might arise). It is worth noting here that the fact that acceptability data are responsive to many kinds of influence does not entail that all those influences must be identified and understood before acceptability data can be put to work in any particular domain, including grammatical theory; we'll come back to this issue below.

In this context, the measurement of judgments of acceptability ought to aim at standard goals of measurement throughout the sciences; observations on judgments of acceptability ought to be as reliable as possible and they should capture the subtlest differentiations that current theory is able to say something about.

Thus the goal of the procedures described in this book is to assess the relative acceptability of sentences. These procedures will assume that sentence acceptability varies continuously. They will not assume or attempt to establish any discrete levels of sentence acceptability. The minimal goal of the procedures is to allow an investigator to determine whether or not there is a (statistically) reliable difference in acceptability between two sentences for a particular population, and, if there is, which of the two is the more acceptable. Further, the procedures should make it possible to compare differences in acceptability; given two pairs of sentences, these procedures should make it possible to determine which pair has the greater difference in acceptability. Because the procedures can be applied to large groups of informants, where a sufficiently large and homogeneous population is available, it should be possible to discriminate the acceptability values of almost any two sentences (although, as indicated earlier, this will be worthwhile only where a theory is available that can make some sense of these discriminations).

In the view adopted here, there is no such thing as an absolutely acceptable or unacceptable sentence, although there might be such a thing as an absolutely grammatical or ungrammatical sentence. No matter how acceptable (or unacceptable) any particular sentence proves to be, these procedures will allow for the possibility that some other sentence will have an even more extreme value. Any attempt to establish criteria for absolute acceptability or unacceptability would confront serious difficulties. Among other things, experience demonstrates that even highly acceptable and theoretically uncontroversial sentences are often judged less than perfect by naive informants. There is evidence that changes of instructions or context as well as other psychological manipulations can shift acceptability values, even for sentences that seem to lie at the extremes of the acceptability scale (see Carroll et al., 1981; Cowart, 1994; Nagata, 1988, 1992, as well as Schütze, 1996, pp. 129-160). Thus, even if we were to assume an underlying binary grammatical mechanism, there are no clear and well-motivated criteria for determining what observed acceptability values are sufficient to establish that a given sentence is (or is not) absolutely acceptable.

There are other empirical phenomena aside from judgments of global acceptability that grammatical theories may be relevant to, such as acceptability under a particular interpretation or scheme of reference relations, or in a given context. The focus here on the overall acceptability of isolated sentences is not meant to slight any of these other kinds of data. Many of the techniques to be described below will also be relevant to the collection of other kinds of judgments. However, questions about the overall acceptability of isolated sentences have played a predominant role in the development of linguistic theory to date. The role of this book is to advocate better methods for collecting that very central kind of evidence.

Another issue needs to be mentioned concerning the relation between grammatical theory and judgments of acceptability. There is a common misconception to this effect: To test grammatical theories by reference to experimentally derived judgment data, it is first necessary to have a fairly thorough theoretical understanding of the processes by which informants produce judgments in experimental settings (i.e., to have answers to the many theoretical questions implicit in the model outlined above). There are at least three reasons to reject this view.

First, the sources of judgment data that emerge from formal experiments are no more obscure than the sources of judgments gathered by way of traditional informal methods. Syntacticians may deploy a thoughtful and thoroughgoing battery of techniques to protect the sentence judgments they make from a variety of extra-grammatical factors. There has been, however, no empirical demonstration of the effectiveness of the training through which most syntacticians acquire these tools, nor any demonstration of the effectiveness of the techniques themselves. Nor is there any tradition of reporting or acknowledging the informal attempts an investigator may make to protect reported judgments against known or suspected distorting factors; this makes it hard for the field as a whole to develop any greater insight into what does and does not work. Informally, it appears that some investigators are good at providing judgments that are relatively free of unwanted influences and are representative of general facts about the target language while other investigators are not. It is up to the good sense and experience of individual readers to tell which is which. So far as their "purity" and relevance are concerned, formal experimental results are certainly no more problematic than the products of traditional methods, while in other respects they are clearly superior.[7]

Second, the important point about judgments of acceptability (however evidence about them is acquired) is not that *all* of the variation in judgments is controlled by the syntactic properties of the target sentences but that *some* of it is. That other factors also play a role is at worst an inconvenience; it is not a bar to making effective use of the phenomenon. Thoughtful research design and modern statistical techniques make it quite practicable to design experiments that, through their structure, isolate those components of variation in judgments that are attributable to (what the theory says ought to be) syntactic manipulations, regardless of what other factors may be contributing to overall variation in judgments in a particular experiment (see Chapter 3). This capacity to reliably associate manipulations with results is all most sciences need to make some progress in theory building.

Third, given that both grammatical theory and psycholinguistics have a legitimate interest in the study of judgments, research would stop if workers in each research tradition were to insist that workers in the other tradition be the first to provide a theory of judgments. If an independent referee were to choose which was to proceed first, grammatical theory would make the better bet because, on the whole, the issues there seem clearer, more tractable, and more amenable to the construction of a richly structured theory.

In short, no issue of "impurity" or lack of insight blocks exploitation of experimentally derived judgment data in the study of grammatical theory. Whether experimental studies of judgments contribute to the development of grammatical theory will depend upon whether investigators find clever and insightful ways to bring the studies to bear on important theoretical issues, not on any intrinsic limitations in this kind of evidence.[8]

One other connection between grammatical theory and the measurement of acceptability should be noted here. Stability is a theory-relative construct; to describe the stability of a phenomenon within a population, we must know what theory is to be applied to it. Most psychological phenomena vary in some degree, and that variability can be quantified in various ways, but whether any particular degree of variability counts as large or small can only be decided relative to specific questions and purposes that derive from a theory. What's needed is that the theory provide categories, distinctions, and descriptive parameters of some sort. Describing the stability of the phenomenon is a matter of comparing the empirical differences in behavior or performance that can be linked to the theory with the random scatter around those theory-linked differences.

To determine how variable syntactic judgments are within a given population, we first find the average empirical difference in acceptability for two sentence types that syntactic theory discriminates and then compare the *variability* of those judgments to the observed difference between the two means. More generally, we look at a wide variety of the kinds of contrasts between sentences that syntactic theory suggests are important. If those differences the theory predicts are generally small relative to the typical variability of the judgments, we might be justified in concluding that judgments are highly variable. On the contrary, the evidence to be reviewed below shows that variability within and between samples of native speakers of American English is generally small relative to the observed differences in acceptability associated with a number of theoretically derived distinctions.

Needless to say, there will be no simple or univocal answers to questions about the stability of grammatical phenomena in speech communities. It seems likely that stability in the judgments in a community will vary by grammatical domain, that binding or ECP effects may show different degrees of stability than parasitic gaps or crossover effects.

We turn now to some direct experimental evidence for the stability of judgments among nonlinguists.

1.3 Evidence of Stability Within Populations

The data presented in this and the next section are intended to show that the kinds of methods described in this book are able to detect stable patterns of judgments in speech communities. These findings will not respond to all the issues raised in the critical literature on judgments. They will show, however, that one population (native speakers of American English) has stable patterns of response with respect to some theoretically significant syntactic issues, and that those patterns of response can be reliably measured via the methods to be described in this book. I will treat all other questions of stability, reliability, and validity as secondary to these issues (see Endnote 1, this chapter). Because the rest of the book will describe in detail the methods used here, a very brief summary will suffice as background to the experiments discussed in this chapter.

The experiments use questionnaires whose materials were constructed according to constraints that typically apply in on-line experiments using sentence stimuli. The materials for each experiment consist of a collection of paradigmlike token sets. Within each token set, all of the sentences (each being a representative of a sentence type) are, as nearly as the design of the experiment will allow, identical to each other. Questionnaires are constructed according to a counterbalancing scheme that ensures that each informant judges exactly one member of each token set, judges representatives of all the sentence types, and judges the same number of sentences in each category. The counterbalancing scheme also ensures that each member of each token set is judged by some subset of the informants in the experiment. Informants judge from three to six or more sentences of each token type. The experimental sentences are randomly mingled with filler sentences of diverse kinds. Wherever possible, the order of presentation of the materials is varied across informants. Informants rate each sentence on some sort of scale, with details varying across experiments. All of these aspects of experimental design and procedure will be discussed in detail later in the book.

All of the results reported in this chapter have been subjected to appropriate statistical tests, although I will report those results only in nontechnical terms within the text of this chapter. Details of statistical tests and results are presented in Appendix B.[9] The main statistical notion I will use here in the main text is "significant" (or "reliable"). In statistics, a significant or reliable difference is one that is unlikely to have occurred by chance. That is, statistical tests such as those used here estimate how likely it is that an observed difference (say, between two means) in the results of an experiment would have occurred if in fact there were no consistent difference between these means in the sampled population. Characterizations such as "significant" or "reliable" are based on explicit criteria; for example, in the psychological and social science literature, a result is usually said to be significant if the probability of it occurring by chance is .05 or less. One or two other statistical notions used later in the chapter are also discussed in Appendix A.

The quantitative results of these experiments will be reported in graphs that will show the relative acceptability of the several sentence types tested. Associated with each data point will be error bars that indicate how much variability there was around the indicated mean (see Figure 1). If the error bars for two means overlap, or come close to it, the two means may not be reliably different. The larger the gap between two means, relative to the size of their error

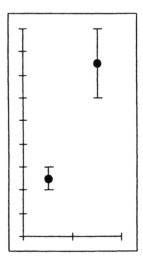

Figure 1. Data points with error bars.

bars, the more likely it is that there is a reliable difference between those means.[10] The vertical scale of all of the graphs used here is defined in terms of standard score (z-score) units. Standard score scales locate each data point relative to the average of all the data covered by a given graph, which is associated with the zero point on the scale. They have the advantage that they capture all of the available information about the relative acceptability of the tested sentence types, while abstracting away from the specifics of the scale used to collect the data (see Appendix A for further discussion).

This section will describe three sets of empirical results relating to different issues in syntactic theory. In each case, the results will show three things. First, some or all of the syntactic contrasts tested prove to be highly stable properties of the sampled population. Second, each experiment corroborates one or more contrasts in acceptability that have been assumed in the syntax literature. Finally, two of the studies reported in this section reveal further aspects of the phenomena in question that have been overlooked (or ignored) in the syntax literature. My purpose in presenting this work here is not to argue for any particular theoretical conclusions but to demonstrate that the procedures employed here can detect reliable differences among the kinds of sentence types that typically matter to grammatical theory.

1.3.1 Subjacency

Sentences such as (1b), (1c), and (1d) appear to involve extraction from a *picture*-NP in a way that violates the subjacency constraint (Chomsky, 1973).[11]

(1) a. Control[12]   Why did the Duchess sell a portrait of Max?
     b. Indefinite   Who did the Duchess sell a portrait of?
     c. Definite   Who did the Duchess sell the portrait of?
     d. Specified   Who did the Duchess sell Max's portrait of?
        Subject

Syntactic accounts of relevant cases have generally assumed that extraction from NPs with specified subjects, as in (1d), is not grammatical, and that extraction from indefinite NPs such as (1b) is grammatical. Opinions have varied on extraction from definite NPs such as (1c). An experimental examination of the relevant acceptability facts used token sets such as (1).[13] Questionnaires designed along the lines discussed above were presented to 88 linguistically naive informants. In this experiment and the next, the same order of materials was used for all informants.[14]

The results are summarized in Figure 2.

The small size of the error bars relative to the large differences between the data points suggests that the pattern is highly reliable, and this impression is confirmed by the statistical results reported in Appendix B. Each of the three rightmost sentence types is reliably less acceptable than the sentence type to its left.

The pattern of these results strongly corroborates the standard assumption that Specified Subject cases such as (1d) are unacceptable. The most interesting feature of the result, however, is not in the contrast between the Control and Specified Subject cases but in the relation of the Indefinite and Definite cases to the two extremes. Although each of the intermediate cases is significantly more acceptable than the Specified Subject cases, both the Indefinite and the Definite cases are reliably less acceptable than the Control case, and reliably different than each other. Insofar as a theory of grammar might be held responsible for explaining these results, that theory must explain why a seemingly quite normal sentence like (1b) should be so sharply distinguished from the Control case.[15]

The next experiment was designed as a follow-up to the first. It provides two new control cases against which to gauge the low

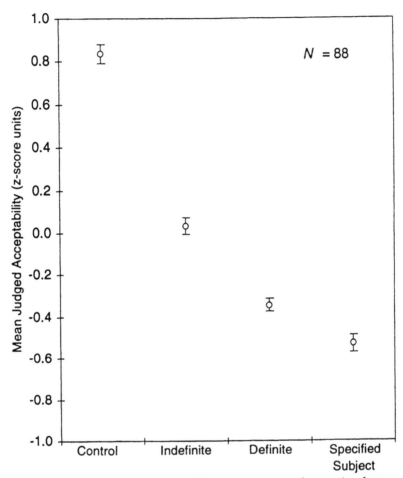

Figure 2. Relative judged acceptability of three cases of extraction from a *picture*-NP.

acceptability of the Indefinite case in (1b) above. The experiment used token sets structured as in (2).

(2) a. Control   Why did the Duchess sell a portrait of Max?
    b. Indefinite   Who did the Duchess sell a portrait of?
       with "of"
    c. Indefinite   Who did the Duchess sell a portrait to?
       with "to"
    d. Specified Subject Who did the Duchess sell Max's portrait to?
       with "to"

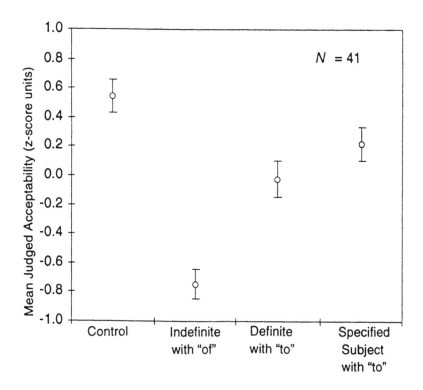

Figure 3. Relative judged acceptability of extractions from *picture*-NPs compared with extraction from a sister to NP.

Here (2a,b) replicate the Control and Indefinite conditions of the first experiment, and (2c) and (2d) provide added relevant points of comparison. Cases such as (2c) are maximally similar to (2b) on the surface but do not involve extraction from within a *picture*-NP. Thus, if the low relative acceptability of the Indefinite cases in the first experiment resulted from informants applying a prescriptive rule against sentences ending in prepositions, (2c) ought to be similarly compromised. The contrast between (2c) and (2d) allows for a comparison to the pattern attained with the superficially similar cases in (1) and provides a third clear case of a class of apparently acceptable sentences against which to compare cases such as (2b).

The procedure was unchanged except that a smaller group of informants was used ($N = 41$).[16] The results of the second experiment are summarized in Figure 3.

As is evident, the Indefinite cases ending in "of" were markedly less acceptable than either the original Control cases or the Indefinite cases ending in "to." As before, the contrast between the Indefinite "of" cases and the Control was significant, but the contrast with the Indefinite "to" cases was also reliable. There was no significant difference between the two cases ending in "to." The overall pattern of results was significant.

Thus sentences such as 2b (and 1b above) seem to be consistently less acceptable than other relevant sentence types. This result may be related to Chomsky's observation that matrix verbs vary in their compatibility with extractions from *picture*-NPs (Chomsky, 1977, pp. 114-115). In any event, it seems that (2b) does not have quite the status usually assumed for it.

These two experiments also provide an empirical basis for considering the question of whether sentence acceptability (as opposed to grammaticality values) varies continuously or by discrete steps. These results strongly support the claim that acceptability varies continuously. Strictly speaking, it is possible that there are two or more distinct patterns in the populations tested here. One might imagine, for example, that all informants in the first experiment reject the Specified Subject cases and all accept the Control cases, but that there is a dialect split on the Indefinite and Definite cases. Averaging across this dialect split gives the appearance of gradedness even though the underlying phenomenon is essentially discrete—indeed, binary. There is, however, no support for this analysis here. One prediction of this analysis is that the variability of informant responses in the Indefinite and Definite cases will be greater than that in the other two. There is no evidence of such differences in either of these experiments; variability around the means is roughly similar across all experimental conditions within each experiment.

1.3.2 "That"-Trace

The third experiment examines the "that"-trace effect described by Chomsky and Lasnik (1977). The standard observation is that there is a certain subject-object asymmetry when "that" is present in cases such as (3). Extraction from either site is acceptable without "that" (3a,b), but only object extraction (3d) is acceptable with "that" (compare with 3c).

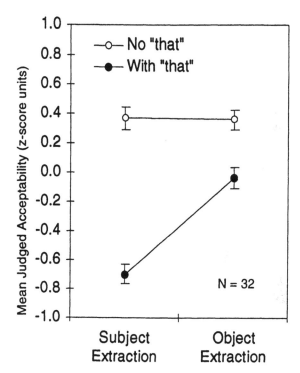

Figure 4. The "that"-trace effect, an interaction between extraction site and the presence of that.

(3)		*No "that"*
	a. Subject Extraction	I wonder who you think likes John.
	b. Object Extraction	I wonder who you think John likes.
		With "that"
	c. Subject Extraction	I wonder who you think that likes John.
	d. Object Extraction	I wonder who you think that John likes.

Data were collected from 32 informants. Eight different orderings of the materials were used.

The results are summarized in Figure 4. There is no difference in acceptability between Subject and Object Extraction in the absence of "that," but there is a reliable difference in the presence of "that." Note also that there is a reliable "that" effect that co-occurs with the "that"-trace effect; both the sentence types containing "that" were less acceptable than the two without "that." This last finding raises the question of how (or whether) the "that"-trace effect might be related to the apparent general bias against all extraction over "that."[17]

The general pattern here is reliable, as the error bars suggest.

1.3.3 Coordination and Binding Theory

The final set of preliminary observations concerns an interaction between reflexives and coordinate NPs. An earlier pilot study indicated that reflexives inside coordinate NPs did not necessarily conform to the Binding Theory (Chomsky, 1981). The token set in (4) was constructed to look for Binding Theory effects where a reflexive appears in first conjunct position inside a coordinate NP.

(4)   *No Coordination*

   a. Local Antecedent   Cathy's parents require that Paul
                                          support himself.

   b. Remote Antecedent   Paul requires that Cathy's parents
                                            support himself.

                                  Simple Coordination

   c. Local Antecedent   Cathy's parents require that Paul
                                          support himself and the child.

   d. Remote Antecedent   Paul requires that Cathy's parents
                                          support himself and the child.

                                  Coordination With "Both"

   e. Local Antecedent   Cathy's parents require that Paul
                                          support both himself and the child.

   f. Remote Antecedent   Paul requires that Cathy's parents
                                          support both himself and the child.

In particular, the question of interest was how informants would evaluate the Remote Antecedent cases, which the Binding Theory would rule ungrammatical. All of the Local Antecedent cases are assumed to be grammatical. The cases incorporating "both" were expected to heighten any effects due to the introduction of coordinate structure by adding a cue at the leading edge of the coordinate NP.

The 43 informants who participated used 24 different orderings of the materials. The results are summarized in Figure 5.

These findings strongly confirm the influence of the Binding Theory in all three pairs of cases. The difference between the two

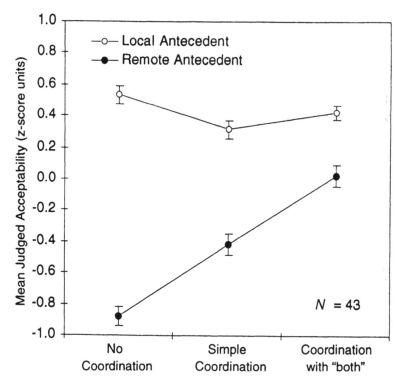

Figure 5. Relative acceptability of sentences containing reflexives with local and remote antecedents by context of the reflexive.

Antecedent Location conditions (local versus remote) is reliable overall and for each of the three coordination conditions.

In addition to the persistent Binding Theory effects, these results also show that reflexives with remote antecedents are significantly more acceptable when the reflexive appears within a coordinate NP. Looking only at the Remote Antecedent cases, there was a significant increase in acceptability from the No Coordination condition to the Simple Coordination condition, and from the Simple Coordination condition to the Both Coordination condition. The question then becomes why it might be that coordinate structures seem to override or partly nullify effects of the Binding Theory (see Frazier & Clifton, 1996, pp. 35-37, for some comments on the theoretical issues these findings raise).[18]

The picture derived from the several experiments described above is unmistakable. Each experiment confirms some well-attested contrast in acceptability, and all of the phenomena are very stable.[19] All of the principal findings are robust enough to be detected with samples much smaller than those used here. There are also some results that are not obviously consistent with current theory or that challenge empirical assumptions that have played some role in grammatical research (e.g., the increased acceptability of reflexives with remote antecedents in coordinate NPs). Although it is far from clear whether any of these findings have important theoretical implications (or what those implications might be), they are reliable aspects of patterns that have otherwise proven interesting and worthy of intensive study. Even if none of the findings reported above is theoretically consequential, it is noteworthy that traditional observational methods have apparently allowed these facts to be misrepresented or overlooked. Taken together, results outlined above provide no support for the suggestion that judgments of acceptability are compromised by extreme variability. There appear to be highly stable patterns of relative sentence acceptability.

1.4 Stability of Responses to Individual Sentences

The reliable differences among judgments of sentence types described above are compatible with different degrees of consistency in the judged acceptability of the individual sentences that fall within those types. This section will present evidence on the stability of speakers' assessments of the relative acceptability of individual sentences.

An indication of the stability of responses to individual sentences appears in Figure 6. Here, 12 sentences were judged by the same 54 informants on two occasions separated by a week or more. The sentences varied widely in acceptability and were presented in one continuous sequence in the same order at both experimental sessions. As is apparent from the graph (and the correlation coefficient), this group of informants gave, on average, almost exactly the same ratings to these 12 sentences in the two sessions.

The procedures to be described in this book are designed to disentangle, insofar as possible, the characteristic acceptability ratings of individual sentences from effects of the contexts in which those sentences occur. Thus, in the ideal case, every informant will see the sentences they are to judge in a different order than does any other informant. This raises the question of how much of the obvious

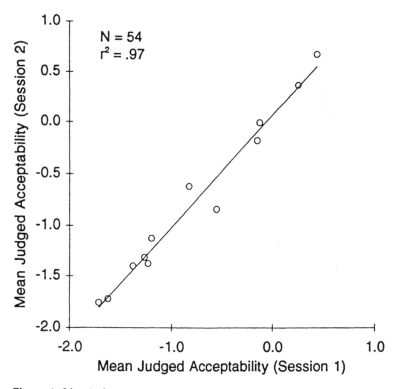

Figure 6. Identical sentences judged on two occasions.

NOTE: Each data point represents the mean of 54 judgments from Session 1 and the mean of 54 judgments from Session 2.

stability evident in Figure 6 is due to the fact that the sentences were presented in the same order on both occasions. The large differences in acceptability among these sentences also help in achieving stable results; contrasts of theoretical interest often will be much more subtle.

To estimate the stability of responses to individual sentences where the order of presentation differs in the two sessions completed by each informant and where, within any one session, various subsets of informants see the materials in different orders, we isolated and analyzed a subset of the data from a "that"-trace experiment (n = 52) in which each informant participated in two sessions.

In this experiment, the filler sentences were identical in the two sessions, differing only in the order in which they were presented. The filler list used was carefully constructed. A preliminary list of highly acceptable sentences was pretested in an earlier experiment and all the sentences getting relatively poor ratings were edited to improve acceptability. Further testing showed that this editing succeeded in producing a list of sentences of relatively uniform high acceptability. This set of filler sentences was then randomly divided so as to isolate a subset of one third of the sentences. These one third of the fillers were then systematically deformed so as to make them conspicuously and dramatically deviant. Further testing showed that this manipulation was successful, yielding the intended strong contrast between the two groups of sentences. These mixed fillers, two thirds highly acceptable, one third very unacceptable, were used in both sessions of the experiment.

This makes for a strong test of the stability of responses to individual sentences because, within each subgroup of filler sentences, the range of differences from sentence to sentence is relatively small. Thus, if there are any differences in acceptability within one of these groups, they ought to be relatively subtle differences, ones that would be difficult to detect and vulnerable to change from session to session.

Similarity across sessions was examined by computing a correlation coefficient for the degree to which the judged acceptability of individual filler sentences in Session 1 predicted the judged acceptability of the same sentences in Session 2. The highly acceptable and the highly unacceptable items were treated separately for these purposes. Figure 7 summarizes the results.

The figure shows that there was a strong relation between the judged acceptability of these sentences in the two sessions. Correlation tests within the two subsets confirmed the impression in Figure 7; there was a strong and reliable correlation between first and second session ratings for both the High Acceptability items and the Low Acceptability items. Thus, even within these two narrow ranges, and with the sentences appearing in different orders at the two sessions, the rated acceptability of individual items was quite similar across the two sessions.

Another frame of reference for considering the stability of responses to individual sentences focuses on the relative acceptability of the several sentences that make up a single token set. That is, we are particularly interested in knowing whether speakers consistently differentiate among the several closely related sentences that make up individual token sets.

Evidence relevant to this issue comes from another "that"-trace study. In this experiment, data were collected from 332 university

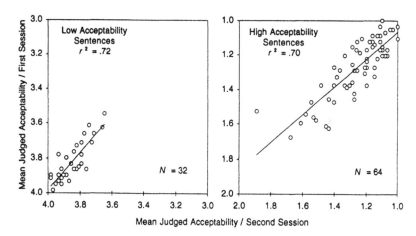

Figure 7. Plots of Session 1 versus Session 2 results for 96 individual filler sentences.

NOTE: A sentence that was given a rating of "1" (highest possible) by all informants in both Session 1 and Session 2 would be represented by a point at the intersection of the "1" lines in the graph for the High Acceptability cases. A sentence given the lowest possible rating ("4") by all informants in both sessions would be indicated at the intersection of the "4" lines in the graph for the Low Acceptability cases. If the results from Session 1 perfectly predicted results from Session 2, then all the data points would lie on the diagonal of one of the graphs. "N" refers to the number of sentences covered by each plot. See Appendix A for interpretation of the r^2 values.

undergraduates at Wayne State College (NE), the University of Alabama at Birmingham, and the University of Southern Maine. The materials for this experiment were somewhat different than those used in the earlier "that"-trace study in that they did not involve indirect questions. A different main clause verb was used for each of the 20 token sets constructed for this study. A sample token set is given in (5).

(5) a. Who do you suppose invited Ann to the circus?
     b. Who do you suppose Ann invited to the circus?
     c. Who do you suppose that invited Ann to the circus?
     d. Who do you suppose that Ann invited to the circus?

The overall results of this study were very similar to those reported in Section 1.3.2 above, except that the gap between Object Extraction cases with and without "that" was smaller, although still reliable overall. There was a small statistically reliable difference between the results from the Alabama cohort and the other two, which resulted from the fact that the gap between the Object Extraction cases with and without "that" did not appear in the results for the Alabama cohort.

To get at evidence on the stability of judgments on individual sentences, the results for each token set were summarized separately for the three cohorts (Nebraska, Alabama, Maine). This produced a table of four means (for the four conditions in [5]) for each of 20 token sets, for each cohort. The 20 token sets themselves and graphs for all of the token sets appear in Appendix D.

Upon inspection of this evidence, two observations were immediately apparent. First, many of the token sets showed distinctive patterns. Although there was a clear "family resemblance" across all the token set graphs, several showed noticeably unique patterns. Second, the patterns for individual token sets were strikingly similar across the three cohorts. Whatever it was that made the pattern for any one token set stand out from the rest in, for example, the Nebraska cohort, it appeared that those same traits were generally evident in the patterns for the other two cohorts.

These findings are illustrated for 4 of the 20 token sets in Figure 8. Note that in the graphs in Figure 8 (as in all those in Appendix E), each data point represents a different subset of informants than do any of the other data points in the same graph. Thus the NT/SE data point (No "that"/Subject Extraction) for the Alabama cohort and the "suppose" token set represents not only a different group of people than do the other two NT/SE data points, but (because of the counterbalancing scheme; see Section 9.5.1) it also represents a different subset of the Alabama cohort than is represented by any of the other three Alabama data points in the same graph. In short, the fact that the patterns are as similar as they are across the three cohorts for each token set reflects a very high degree of similarity across the three subpopulations represented here. The three cohorts do not agree merely by sentence type (liking NT/SE sentences and rejecting WT/SE sentences); rather, they agree, for the most part, token set by token set and sentence by sentence.

1.4.1 Overview of Evidence

Taken together, the results presented in this chapter show clearly that there is a stable natural phenomenon of sentence acceptability; we find that for all of the syntactic phenomena considered here, native speakers of American English exhibit stable, clear-cut patterns of acceptability differences across sentence types. Although these patterns are of the kind commonly discussed in the syntax

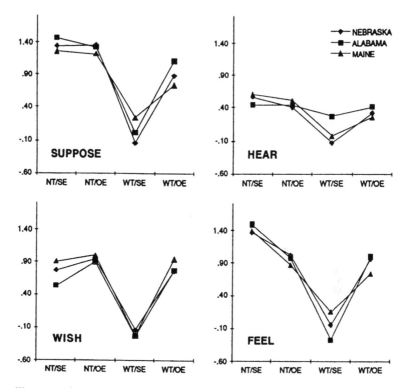

Figure 8. Sentence by sentence mean judged acceptability data for four token sets in a "that"-trace experiment.

NOTE: Each line in each graph represents data collected from informants at a different site (Nebraska, Alabama, Maine). NT/SE = No "that," Subject Extraction cases; WT/OE = With "that," Object Extraction cases; and so on. Each data point is the standardized mean (see Appendix A) of all the responses for that cohort for that sentence. Each of the four token sets was based on the verb indicated in the graph for that token set.

literature, these results also show that there are sometimes details of these patterns that have gone unnoticed or underestimated in syntactic research. The evidence reviewed above also demonstrates that there are practical experimental methods by which the phenomenon of sentence acceptability can be measured and assessed.

1.5 Outline of the Book

This chapter has stressed stability; the next will stress variability. At least where the judgments of naive informants are concerned, it is the details of variability in those data that provide the strongest motivation for relying on formal experimental procedures in assessing acceptability phenomena. Chapter 3 is the keystone of the rest of the book. It introduces the notion of variance control and reviews the major sources of variance that need to be controlled in experiments on acceptability. It lays out the logic underlying experiments like those described above. The chapter also considers constraints on the form that sentence materials may take and some issues related to the construction of experimental and filler materials. With this material as background, investigators will have a better sense of what the essential features are of the procedures discussed below, and be better equipped to modify those procedures appropriately when the need arises. Chapter 4 considers some of the different kinds of information that syntactic investigators may seek and the issues that arise in getting at that information experimentally. Alternative modes of presenting sentences to informants and of collecting and measuring their responses are reviewed in Chapters 5 and 6, respectively. Chapters 7 and 8 discuss sampling and other issues linked to the actual execution of experimental procedures. Many issues arise in connection with the organization of questionnaires, and Chapter 9 covers this topic in some detail. Recovering the data from an experiment and initial statistical summaries are discussed in Chapters 10 and 9 while Chapter 12 reviews some more specialized issues in statistics and measurement. Finally, Appendix C is a tutorial intended to introduce spreadsheet novices to the functions in Excel (a spreadsheet program) that are most useful for creating and analyzing acceptability experiments.

Notes

1. In the context of psychometrics especially, psychologists are often concerned with the reliability of individual measurements, that is, with the consistency of repeated measurements on the same individual. Needless to say, some degree of reliability in this individual sense is a prerequisite for obtaining reliable evidence on populations, but experimental science focusing on the traits of populations can proceed with cruder instruments than those that are required when the goal of measurement is to characterize one particular individual (especially where that measurement may have practical consequences for the individual).

The concept of reliability is also connected with questions about whether measurements accurately reflect the true state (i.e., true score) of the targeted property of the individual. Measurements may be reliable (in the sense of consistent) and yet systematically distort the characteristic they are meant to measure (giving, for example, values that are consistently too high or too low in particular parts of the range of the measurement). Reliability is also connected with validity, questions about what it is that a particular psychological test actually measures (e.g., to what extent IQ is a measure of a cognitive trait rather than an inadvertent index of socioeconomic background). Schütze's Chapter 3 (1996) is essentially a review of the literature on validity as it relates to judgments.

All of these issues are obviously relevant to work with judgments in linguistics, but collecting reliable and scientifically useful data on patterns of sentence acceptability in speech communities does not require the prior resolution of any questions of these kinds. Although I will keep to the relatively informal usages of the linguistic literature when any of these issues come up, I will try to indicate clearly which notion of stability is relevant wherever we need to consider matters other than stable measures of the characteristics of linguistic communities.

2. Newmeyer (1983) argues that most of these disagreements are not about the facts of acceptability. He suggests that in several cases judgments were constant, but conflicts among theorists on how various sources of unacceptability should be accounted for drove changes in the status ascribed to certain sentences.

3. This sample of papers includes those that were identified in a search of the PsychINFO database (American Psychological Association). The search target was specified as follows: grammatical? (1n) judgment?. This was intended to select all papers whose database entry included adjacent instances (in either order) of the target terms or their variants.

4. Nagata (1987a, 1987b, 1988, 1989a, 1989b, 1989c, 1989d) notwithstanding, it appears to be essential to the nature of sentences (and human responses to them) that they have identities in ways that flashes of light do not. Linguists and psychologists, in taking an interest in the structure of language, naturally view sentences as categories and see particular utterances as instances of those categories. From the standpoint of day-to-day usage, however, repeating sentences seems to have some status akin to re-eating a meal; the food wasn't quite right, or the conversation took a bad turn, so we hit the rewind button and did it again on the spot. Sentences seem to be ordinarily experienced as unique and unrepeatable events. Although we can individuate flashes of light (or sounds, or smells, or the like) by identifying each with a time, this seems somehow contrary to the ordinary experience of such events. From a psychological point of view, it seems all the light that flows from a bulb is part of the same quantity or entity; individuating particular flashes feels a bit like giving different personal names to a person's left arm, right arm, left ear, and so on. In short, it does serious violence to the ordinary way of relating to sentences to ask informants to judge the same sentence many times. This does not mean, of course, that repeated presentations in experimental settings are unthinkable, but it does raise questions about how to relate those events to more typical uses of sentences.

5. I am, with some trepidation, attempting here to summarize a view of these issues that emerges in various of Chomsky's writings over many years. Readers who wish to consider the issues in more detail should consult Schütze (1996), especially his Chapter 2, which cites the various relevant works of Chomsky's.

6. Bever and his colleagues (Bever, 1974; Bever & Carroll, 1981; Gerken & Bever, 1986; Katz & Bever, 1976; see also Schütze, 1996, pp. 62-70) have argued that there are very good reasons to explain evidence of gradedness in judgments solely by reference to performance systems while maintaining a discrete model of the grammar.

7. Formal methods have the distinct advantage that they are public and replicable. They allow for productive ways of resolving data disputes where standard informal methods do not. With traditional methods, disputes about data can easily become dead-ends, regardless of the actual quality of the data in question.

8. Even if linguists have wildly misconstrued the origin of judgments (suppose, as some would claim, there is simply no distinct cognitive subsystem that has properties or roles like those assigned to grammars), evidence of stable patterns of judgments in speech communities is likely to be scientifically important. If the phenomena of acceptability are stable and richly structured in the ways that current evidence suggests they are, accounting for these facts will still stand as an important challenge for cognitive theory.

9. Appendix A provides a brief introduction to the various statistical concepts and procedures that are cited or used in Appendix B or elsewhere in the book.

10. The size of the error bars in the graphs is determined by the standard error of the mean, a notion that is discussed in Appendix A.

11. Chomsky's account of these cases changed substantially in the "Barriers" framework (1986).

12. *Control* is used here in the sense of "control group."

13. Preliminary results of this and the next experiment were reported previously (Cowart, 1989a, 1989b). The design for this experiment called for 24 items but 1 item was deleted by error.

14. The experiment was executed in collaboration with Diana Smetters.

15. It should be noted that the result is averaged over many sentences. The reported result is not for the particular example sentences in (1). Section 1.4 and Appendix E provide some information on sentence-by-sentence differences in a "that"-trace experiment. In the subjacency experiments described in this section, there may be important effects associated with individual verbs.

16. The experiment was conducted by a student, Ken Williams, as part of an M.A. thesis project. No analysis on token sets was done.

17. In subsequent work on this phenomenon, we have replicated this difference at almost every opportunity, although the magnitude of the difference is usually less than what is seen here.

18. Ross (1970) and Zribi-Hertz (1989) discuss cases suggestive of the phenomenon observed here.

19. All of the phenomena described above emerged in the course of longer-term investigations that have demonstrated the same or similar effects several times. In the case of the "that"-trace phenomena, as we'll see, very similar patterns have been detected in widely separated populations around the United States.

2

Error Variance
in Sentence
Judgments

In countless psychophysical, cognitive, and physical tasks, human performance is characterized by a random scatter of individual observations around a more or less stable mean. In statistics, this scatter is termed *error variance* and it is ubiquitous in observations of human performance. The purpose of this chapter is to provide a clearer picture of the magnitude of error variance in sentence judgments and to consider its significance for the problem of getting reliable information about patterns of judgments in the general population. Although the results described in Chapter 1 demonstrate a high degree of stability in a number of judgment phenomena, a closer examination of these and other similar studies also reveals much greater error variance affecting individual responses than traditional linguistic approaches to judgments have generally allowed for.

Standard methods in syntactic research reflect relatively little concern with the role of error variance in judgments of sentence acceptability. This is easily seen in the way that linguists have sometimes approached experimental work on judgments. Hill's (1961) paper reports the responses of individual informants in some detail, noting considerable divergence around points where it seems Chomsky (1957) anticipated agreement. Notably, however, even though he seemed to be probing for evidence counter to Chomsky's empirical assumptions, it does not seem to have occurred to Hill to present the sample sentences to his informants a second time. Although Ross's (1979) study mentions in passing the question of "repeatability" in connection with asking his informants to rate their confidence in the judgments they provide, he apparently did not do any explicit checks of repeatability. Whatever doubts these investigators might have harbored about the reliability of judgment data, they did not check to see whether informants would agree with themselves upon doing the same questionnaire a few weeks or months later. In both these cases, the investigators behaved as though each response from each informant was (or was close to) a definitive representation of that informant's attitude toward that sentence and the sentence type it represents.

In typical psychological studies, error variance is assumed; investigators routinely collect numbers of observations from each participant, often ask each participant to respond to each stimulus many times, and report the procedural and/or statistical methods used to control error variance. Standard practice recognizes that individual observations are not reliable, and sophisticated practitioners may evaluate findings differently according to their confidence in the means employed to control error variance. The fact that the syntax literature is characterized by consistent inattention to the methods by which sentence judgments are gathered and summarized is not compatible with due concern for the role of error variance.

Nevertheless, error variance is present in judgments of acceptability. This is easily seen in a more detailed analysis of the "that"-trace study mentioned in Section 1.4 above (although the same point could be made with data from almost any experimental study of judgments). In this study, each informant judged five different representatives of each of the four sentence type categories shown in (6).

(6) a. Who do you suppose invited Ann to the circus?
   b. Who do you suppose Ann invited to the circus?
   c. Who do you suppose that invited Ann to the circus?
   d. Who do you suppose that Ann invited to the circus?

A variant of a standard psychophysical scaling method (see Section 6.2) was used to express the relative acceptability of individual sentences. As usual, the mean of each informant's responses within each sentence type category was taken as the index of the informant's attitude toward that category.

A follow-up analysis of this study isolated a subset of 88 informants who had all judged the same experimental and filler sentences (although in one of two different orders). The follow-up analysis calculated the range between the informant's highest and lowest ratings within each sentence type (e.g., With "that"/Object Extraction) and the mean rating within each category. This made it possible to construct a rough index of the size of the "that"-trace effect for each informant.[1] This measure was then compared with the range of ratings within various sentence type categories.

This analysis reveals what might appear to be an extraordinary degree of inconsistency in informant responses; for roughly 90% of the informants, the average range of variation *within* sentence type categories exceeded the difference between the "that"-trace violations (6c) and the average of the other three types. Indeed, on average, for individual informants the mean range *within* categories was more than 80% larger than the size of the "that"-trace effect. The "that"-trace effect was smaller than the average range within categories even for half of the 10 informants who showed the least overall variation within categories. In short, for most informants a great many of their individual sentence judgments were unrepresentative of the average acceptability of the category from which the sentence was drawn.

The consequences of this degree of variability in individual responses are illustrated by the data from five informants shown in Figure 9. An informant can be said to show the "that"-trace effect if the average of the five bars in the With "that"/Subject Extraction is lower than the average of the bars in the other three graphs. Informant 1 is perhaps the single "best" informant in this subset, showing very little variation within each sentence type category and a clear difference between the "that"-trace violations (With "that"/Subject Extraction) and the other three types. Informant 2 is much more like

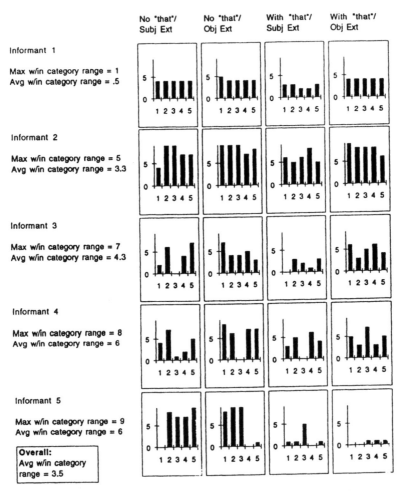

Figure 9. Within-category variation in response for individual informants.

NOTE: Each row of graphs represents data from one informant. Each graph shows the informant's responses to all five of the sentences of a particular type that the informant judged. Each bar in one of the graphs represents the informant's response on one sentence. The sentence types are identified at the top of each column of graphs. The vertical axis of the graphs shows the rating scale, running from 0 to 9.

the typical case. Here, although there is a difference in average response between the "that"-trace violations and the other three (difference = 1.8), the range of variation within every sentence type category exceeds this difference (5, 2, 3, 3, respectively). Furthermore, there were many more variable informants who showed patterns like those seen in Informants 3, 4, and 5. Although the first two of these informants shows the "that"-trace effect overall, the range of variation within sentence categories overwhelms average between-categories differences in every case.

This degree of error variance, however, did not obscure the overall finding. Informants gave high ratings to the (6a) and (6b) sentences, slightly (but reliably) lower ratings to the (6d) sentences, and far lower ratings to the (6c) sentences. The overall pattern was highly reliable.[2]

In short, when results were averaged across the several sentences to which each informant responded and averaged across informants, the error variance demonstrated earlier was not sufficient to overcome or seriously obscure the underlying evidence of the "that"-trace effect. Similar patterns of substantial error variance accompanied by clear and consistent overall patterns have been found for other syntactic phenomena as well.

A further indication of the magnitude of error variance in judgments comes from another "that"-trace experiment in which 21 informants (out of a far larger sample) responded to exactly the same questionnaire on each of two occasions a week or more apart. This contrasts with the previous study where the informants saw the target sentences in two different orders. These questionnaires included only three sentences of each syntactic type. Nevertheless, the general "that"-trace effect evident in the full experiment and earlier studies was reliably replicated with this small subset of informants.[3] On the other hand, an informant's means for the four experimental conditions from the first session were generally poor predictors of that informant's means from the second session (see Figure 10). As we saw earlier, highly stable patterns may be discernible in data from a group of informants without those same patterns being readily detectable in the results of individual informants.

These findings indicate that there is normally more than enough error variance in judgments of sentence acceptability given by naive informants to make the control of this variance a proper concern of any reader of proffered general claims about the relative acceptability of sentence types. Nevertheless, as the data reviewed in Chapter 1 indicate, this error variance is easily controlled by standard tools of experiment design and statistical analysis, so long as these tools are properly applied.[4]

It is not clear how the judgment performance of experts compares with that of typical naive informants. It may be that particular

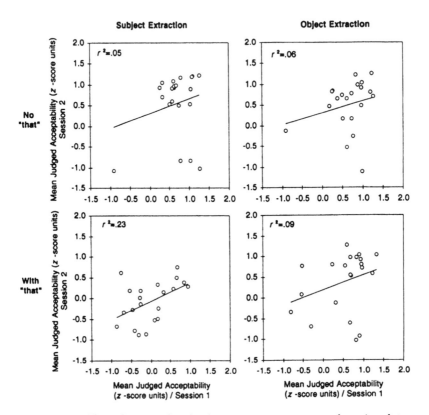

Figure 10. These four graphs plot first session versus second session data for 21 informants who were given exactly the same version of a "that"-trace questionnaire on each of two occasions.

NOTE: At each session, each informant judged the same three sentences in each experimental condition (e.g., the No "that"/Subject Extraction condition). The data point representing each informant in each graph is determined by the mean of the informant's three responses at the first session (X axis) and the mean of the informant's three responses on the same three sentences at the second session (Y axis). If informants had given the same or nearly the same responses at both sessions, all data points would lie at or near the diagonal in each plot. The r^2 values estimate the share of variance in the second session that can be explained by reference to the data from the first session.

individuals (through specialized training, experience, exceptional insight, or sensitivity) are able to reliably estimate general patterns of sentence acceptability in a community. There is, however, usually no way to tell whether a particular pattern of judgments offered by an individual is representative of the target population apart from applying experimental procedures like those used here.

The procedures described in this book assume the existence of error variance in sentence judgments and apply various measures to control that variance. The most important of these measures are the use of multiple informants and multiple instances of any sentence type whose acceptability is to be estimated. The general problem of designing experiments on judgments that properly account for the existence of error variance and the other constraints peculiar to studies of sentence materials is considered in the next chapter.

Notes

1. The difference between the informant's average rating for the With "that"/ Subject Extraction cases and the average of the other three categories was taken as the measure of the "that"-trace effect for each informant.

2. From this point on in the text, when needed, statistical results will be reported in endnotes. Readers unfamiliar with the tests reported should consult Appendix A.

There was a reliable interaction between the Presence or Absence of "that" and the Extraction Site factors, $F_1(1, 331) = 361$, $p < .001$. Both the main effects were also significant, $F_1(1, 331) = 690$, $p < .001$, for "that," and $F_1(1, 331) = 281$, $p < .001$, for Extraction Site. Various formal and informal methods suggest that the effects were robust enough to be tested with samples as small as eight informants without undue risk ($\approx .25$) of a Type II error. We'll return to sample size issues in Chapter 9.

3. The "that" versus Extraction Site interaction was reliable, $F_1(1, 20) = 11.4$, $p < .01$, as was the main effects of "that," $F_1(1, 20) = 11.1$, $p < .01$, and Extraction Site, $F_1(1, 20) = 11.0$, $p < .01$.

4. Readers unfamiliar with the theory of measurement and reliability may find it paradoxical that a measurement procedure, such as giving acceptability judgments for sentences, can give reliable evidence about the relative acceptability of sentences or sentence types for a population while providing very unstable information about the individual informants in the sample on which those general findings are based. There is no paradox. What is happening is simply that the analysis of the experiment as a whole is aggregating weak information gleaned from the individual informants to provide a strong indication of the state of affairs in the target population. If there were a way to subject each informant to a measurement effort as intensive as that applied to the full sample (e.g., collecting 50 responses on every target sentence), it is likely that we could acquire information about each informant roughly as reliable as that we are able to obtain for a population from a sample.

A corollary is that having achieved reliable measurement of a population via a sample does not give evidence that we have achieved reliable measurement of individuals that make up the sample. This raises some concerns because when linguists collect experimental data, they are often tempted to examine and comment on the results for individual informants. Such efforts ought to be reserved for cases where the reliability of the measurement procedure (vis-à-vis individual informants) has been established. As of now, linguists have available no experimental procedure for gathering judgment data that meets this criterion.

3

Designing
Experiments
on Acceptability

We do experiments to estimate the properties of a population on the basis of tests applied to a sample drawn from that population.

The sample is always divided in some fashion so that we can compare the effects of one experimental condition against another. In a minimal psychological experiment, the sample is divided into a test group and a control group, with some "treatment" being applied to the test group. We expect to learn something about the effects of the treatment *in the population* by looking for measurable differences between the test and control groups after the treatment has been applied.

Unfortunately, we can expect that there will almost always be some difference between the two groups—even if we do nothing at all except select and measure them. Thus the central problem in the interpretation of experiments is deciding when a difference between groups within a sample is large enough to warrant the inference that there is also a difference in the population the sample represents.

The statistical approach to this problem aims to provide explicit rational control of the *frequency* of errors in this process. It holds out no prospect of assurance, except the assurance that, under certain assumptions, no more than some predetermined proportion of the inferences we draw in interpreting experiments will lead to error.

This level of control is achieved by using the normal random scatter of observations that occurs within almost all samples as a kind of yardstick against which to measure the differences among groups or conditions. The background scatter, error variance, will spontaneously produce differences between test and control groups even without experimental interventions. Through careful statistical modeling of error variance, however, we can determine how often purely accidental differences of various sizes will arise. On the basis of these estimates, we can determine how likely it is that a particular observed difference between two groups arose purely by chance. If the observed difference is, by this analysis, sufficiently unlikely to have come about solely by chance, we may be warranted in drawing the inference that there is a real difference in the population corresponding to the difference between the groups in an experiment.

Another way to describe the same strategy is to say that we will use within groups variance (the error variance that we find within any sample of individuals) as a basis for gauging the size of the between groups variance (the difference between groups that is, potentially, the product of our experimental manipulation).

There are two problems for research design that arise in this context. The tests and activities within an experiment must be structured in some way to produce differences between groups. If successful, this activity will produce reliable differences that will support inferences about the relevant population. However, reliable differences are of little scientific interest unless we can determine how they came about in the experiment. Thus the second and more challenging aspect of research design is the task of ensuring the meaningfulness of the results achieved in experimental studies.

The fundamental work that research design must do to achieve meaningful results is to control variance. In many experiments (including ones on judgments), every response may be unique and the responses may spread over a wide range. These responses are potentially useful exactly because they differ from each other, provided that some of this variability is under the experimenter's control. Research design aims to impose structure on the variability in experimental results so that observed differences can be given some theoretical interpretation.

Because the statistical tests that are relevant to the problems under consideration here are defined around the technical concept of "variance," it will be helpful to review this notion in a little detail. As we'll see, effective design aims at exercising thorough experimental (i.e., procedural) and statistical control of three particular kinds of variance.

3.1 Variance and Variance Partitioning

A statistical summary of a collection of scores will generally need to indicate both the "location" of the collection of scores (e.g., their mean or average) and the degree to which the scores are spread out around that mean. One fairly obvious way to represent the "spread-outness" of the scores would be to subtract the mean of the full set of scores from each individual score and take the average of these *difference* scores. Because of the way the mean is defined, however, the sum and (therefore) the average of the difference scores will always be zero. This difficulty is overcome by squaring each difference score (which makes them all positive) before taking their average. This procedure is illustrated in the two columns to the right of the column of judgment responses in Table 1. The mean of the squared difference scores is termed the *variance* of the full set of scores.

Designing a useful experiment can be seen as finding a way to partition this value, the total variance of the set of scores, into two or more components.

Suppose, for example, that the 20-judgment responses were obtained in the following way. The first 10 scores represent the responses of 10 informants who judged Sentence A, and the second 10 represent informants who judged a different sentence, Sentence B. As illustrated in the middle and rightmost columns of Table 1, we can now use the mean for each group of informants to partition the total variance calculated earlier.

This partitioning is achieved first by using the mean for each group, instead of the overall mean, to calculate the difference and

Table 1 Partitioning the variance for a set of scores.

	Judgment Responses	Each Individual response compared to the grand mean		Each Individual response compared to the Individual's group mean		Each Individual's group mean compared to the grand mean	
		Difference Score	Squared Difference Score	Difference Score	Squared Difference Score	Difference Score	Squared Difference Score
Sentence A Responses	2	-2.95	8.70	-1.60	2.56	-1.35	1.82
	2	-2.95	8.70	-1.60	2.56	-1.35	1.82
	6	1.05	1.10	2.40	5.76	-1.35	1.82
	5	0.05	0.00	1.40	1.96	-1.35	1.82
	6	1.05	1.10	2.40	5.76	-1.35	1.82
Sum	3	-1.95	3.80	-0.60	0.36	-1.35	1.82
36	5	0.05	0.00	1.40	1.96	-1.35	1.82
Group Mean	3	-1.95	3.80	-0.60	0.36	-1.35	1.82
3.60	1	-3.95	15.60	-2.60	6.76	-1.35	1.82
	3	-1.95	3.80	-0.60	0.36	-1.35	1.82
Sentence B Responses	4	-0.95	0.90	-2.30	5.29	1.35	1.82
	4	-0.95	0.90	-2.30	5.29	1.35	1.82
	3	-1.95	3.80	-3.30	10.89	1.35	1.82
	9	4.05	16.40	2.70	7.29	1.35	1.82
	3	-1.95	3.80	-3.30	10.89	1.35	1.82
	9	4.05	16.40	2.70	7.29	1.35	1.82
Sum	6	1.05	1.10	-0.30	0.09	1.35	1.82
63	9	4.05	16.40	2.70	7.29	1.35	1.82
Group Mean	7	2.05	4.20	0.70	0.49	1.35	1.82
6.30	9	4.05	16.40	2.70	7.29	1.35	1.82

All Responses
Sum
99
Grand Mean
4.95

		Each Individual response compared to the grand mean	Each Individual response compared to the Individual's group mean	Each Individual's group mean compared to the grand mean
	Sum of Difference Scores	0.00	0.00	0.00
(Sum of Squared Differences Scores)	Sum of Squares	126.95 =	90.50 +	36.45
(Mean of Squared Difference Scores)	Variance	6.35 =	4.53 +	1.82
		Total Variance =	Within Groups Variance +	Between Groups Variance

NOTE: Each row in the main body of the table represents a single informant. The informants are divided into two groups, each of which includes ten individuals who supplied one judgment response each. The first column of difference scores compares the individual's response to the grand mean (5.3). The second column of difference scores compares each informant's judgment response to the mean for that informant's group (3.90 for the first group and 6.70 for the second). Finally, the rightmost column of difference scores shows the difference between the mean for the informant's group and the grand mean. Thus, for the first ten informants this difference score is always 3.90 – 5.3 = –1.40, and for the second it is 6.70 – 5.3 = 1.40. Toward the bottom of the table, each value in the Sum of Squares row shows the sum of the *squared* difference values in the same column. The values in the variance row are obtained by dividing the values in the Sum of Squares row by the number of individuals (20). Crucially, the sum of the Within Groups and Between Groups Variances equals the Total Variance. This example demonstrates the general logic of variance partitioning, but not its actual application in statistical tests. In statistical tests, the goal is to *estimate* relevant parameters for a population by way of data taken from a sample drawn from that population. This complicates the logic and the math, but the underlying concept remains the same.

squared difference values for each individual score within each group. This removes the effects of the overall difference between the two groups from the calculation of the squared difference value for each score. It is as though every informant is part of the same group judging the same sentence. Thus the variance that remains is just the error variance discussed in the previous chapter, the variance that arises mostly from the ordinary meaningless scatter of scores around any mean. Another, somewhat more transparent, term for this variance is *within groups variance* and this is what is used in Table 1.

The term *error variance* notwithstanding, it could be that all of this variance is due to orderly processes and is ultimately explainable. However, as Kerlinger (1973, p. 78) suggests, our ignorance of its sources and our inability to control much of it—at least in any one experiment—forces us to regard it as meaningless. It should be noted, however, that the role of error variance is quite benign, despite the need to control and minimize it in experimental design. It is precisely error variance that most statistical tests use as the yardstick against which experimental effects are measured and reliability estimated. That is, what many common statistical tests do is estimate the overall stability of the sampled population from the measure of error variance. This provides an index of how large differences between groups must be to be *un*likely to have occurred by chance.

Turning to the experimental effects in the example in Table 1, it is now possible to calculate a further variance component based directly on the means for Sentence A and Sentence B. The mean for each of the two groups is shown at the left of Table 1. In the rightmost two columns of the table, we calculate the difference between each informant's group mean and the overall mean of the full data set, as well as the square of this difference value. This, of course, is highly redundant because the group mean does not vary within the group. Just as we did with the squared difference values for the individual scores, we take the mean of the squared difference values for the group means at the bottom of the rightmost column. This is our second component of the total variance in the experiment. This component reflects the experimental effect, the differences in judgments due to the differences between Sentence A and Sentence B, and is usually called *between groups variance*.

We can demonstrate that this procedure in fact consists in a partitioning of the variance in the entire data set by adding up the *between groups variance* and the *within groups variance*; the sum of these variances is equal to the *total variance*.

The application of variance partitioning in actual statistical tests involves many complexities that need not concern us here. Among other things, variances computed in typical statistical tests are understood as estimates of variances in the population from which the sample is drawn. This complicates various aspects of the calculation. Analysis of variance techniques also allows many different independent comparisons to be made within one experiment. That is, factorial designs allow simultaneous tests on two or more different treatments (e.g., the Sentence A/Sentence B contrast) within one experiment. Despite the added mathematical complexity these extensions involve, the underlying logic of variance partitioning remains essentially the same.

3.2 Experiment Design

To review, the art of experiment design consists in controlling variance. There are two reasons for this. First, it is the ratio of the between groups variance and within groups variance that will ultimately decide questions about the reliability of the result. If the experimenter does not provide a manipulation that produces a sufficiently large difference between the means of the groups, there will (from a statistical point of view) be no result at all. Second, it is the appropriateness of the manipulations that induce differences between the group means and the steps taken to ensure that *only* these differences distinguish the groups that will determine the meaningfulness and validity of the result.

For the purposes of this discussion, I will look at experimental design mostly as a problem of manipulating certain categorical variables (e.g., Sentence Type A versus Sentence Type B) so as to induce effects on a continuous variable (acceptability). A finer differentiation of parameters will be needed eventually, but this distinction should serve well enough here.

In designing an experiment, it is useful to consider three kinds of variance that must be controlled. The first two we've already encountered.

Between groups variance is due to the experimental manipulations constructed by the experimenter. In the example in Table 1, it is the variance due to the difference between Sentence A and Sentence B. The design problem for between groups variance is to ensure that whatever difference is observed is in fact due to the intended factor.

Within group variance, the second type relevant here, is generally inevitable, ultimately benign, and not particularly difficult to manage so long as its existence and approximate magnitude are appropriately recognized in the design of an experiment.

The third kind of variance might be termed *extraneous systematic variance*. This consists of any part of the variance in the experiment that is orderly, but not the part of the variance that the experimenter means to manipulate. If, for example, long sentences are judged less acceptable than short ones, and if the sentences in some experimental condition, Condition A, are consistently shorter than those in Condition B, then A may be judged better than B for different reasons than the experimenter intends. We say that the contrast between Conditions A and B is confounded; any difference we observe in connection with this contrast may be due to *either* the syntactic difference between them or to the length difference. Confounding can make it impossible to derive any interesting or useful conclusion from an experimental result. Control of extraneous systematic variance is an extremely important issue in the design of experiments on sentence materials because there seem to be many different ways that it can arise. Section 3.3 will address this issue in detail.

Extraneous variance can also be an issue in the control of error variance. When, for example, each group of informants in an experiment consists of two different kinds of persons (in equal proportions), there may be no issue of confounding, but there may be a problem all the same. As noted, detecting statistically reliable differences among experimental conditions depends ultimately on the ratio of between groups and within groups variance. If there are large systematic differences among two different types of persons (e.g., speakers of two different dialects), it may be worthwhile to control this factor so as to reduce error variance. If, for example, the population from which a particular group of informants is selected includes members of two different dialect communities who have differing responses to the experimental stimuli, the experimenter has two choices. The experimenter can select each group of informants in such a way as to ensure that approximately equal numbers of members of the two communities appear in each group of informants. This should ensure that the difference between members of the two communities will have no untoward effect on the experiment. Alternatively, the experimenter might choose to select informants from only one of the two communities, or run two parallel experiments using informants from just one of the communities in each of the two procedures. These latter alternatives have the advantage of reducing the total error variance in the experiment, which improves the experimenter's opportunity to detect real differences associated with the intended manipulations.

One of the key challenges in designing meaningful and interesting experiments is to ensure that any systematic variance in the experiment is either appropriately identified and directly manipulated or effectively neutralized and submerged within the error variance in the experiment. As we'll see, the main focus of this effort in the design of experiments on acceptability is directed toward the design of the materials that will represent the various experimental conditions. In an experiment on judgments, by far the most likely source of extraneous systematic variance lies in the opportunity to inadvertently introduce differences between the materials in various conditions.

Apart from the sentence materials themselves, the main likely sources of extraneous systematic variance in experiments on sentence judgments are the ordering of those materials and differences among informants. Each of these factors will be considered below.

3.3 Designing and Constructing Sentence Materials

For experiments on syntax or syntactic processing issues, the design and execution of sentence materials largely determines what, if anything, the result will mean.

What makes the materials so critical is that there are many intricately interacting systematic factors affecting judgments of individual sentences. There is evidence suggesting that an informant's response to an individual sentence may be affected by many different lexical, syntactic, semantic, and pragmatic factors, together with an assortment of extralinguistic influences that become haphazardly associated with linguistic materials or structures. In particular, the frequency and/or familiarity of the lexical items, the length of those items, the semantic properties of each item, and each item's associations with other items and with miscellaneous facets of the informant's personal history can affect informant response. Syntactic factors such as clausal structure, the specific devices that are used to implement various syntactic roles (e.g., choice of complementizer or relative pronoun), the complexity of a structure, the familiarity or frequency of a structure, and parsability can all influence judgments. Semantic factors such as the use of negation or the logical complexity of a sentence (e.g., "I couldn't fail to disagree with you less"),[1] or pragmatic factors having to do with what presuppositions or entailments the informant is (or is not) sensitive to may affect judgments. The interpretation the informant assigns to the sentence may have unpredictable associations with the informant's life history that can substantially affect judged acceptability. In short, any one person's response to any one sentence is usually massively confounded.

These observations are hardly surprising. Linguists have long been aware that judgments can be affected by many factors having little or no relevance to syntax. Although various steps have been taken to try to control these extrasyntactic influences, the effectiveness of these efforts has never been demonstrated.

The procedures described in this book differ from more typical linguistic approaches to this problem. Rather than attempting to suppress extrasyntactic influences, these procedures control these influences by trying to spread them as uniformly as possible across all the sentence types to be tested, and by assuming that (because each sentence may be influenced by a unique assortment of the factors listed above) no one sentence of a given syntactic type is an ideal representative of that type. The procedures described here assume that sentence judgments are subject to a host of factors contributing to extraneous systematic variance. The factors enumerated above are for the most part, apparently, principled and consistent in their effects, but many are not among the kind of systematic factors that are thought to matter to syntax. Thus the goal of experiment design here is to ensure that these miscellaneous systematic but theoretically irrelevant influences do not inadvertently align with whatever factors are of syntactic interest in a particular experiment. If two sentences are meant to implement a contrast between, say, violating or not violating the subjacency constraint, the goal here is to ensure that, as nearly as possible, it is only subjacency that differentiates the two cases—all other lexical, syntactic, semantic, pragmatic, and miscellaneous psychological factors being uniformly distributed across the two sentences.

This ideal, of course, can be very hard to attain in a variety of circumstances, so it is often helpful to employ what are called factorial designs, as illustrated with the "that"-trace materials in Table 2. The

Table 2 A factorial presentation of materials for a "that"-trace study.

	Presence/absence of "that"	
	Without "that"	With "that"
Extraction Site		
Subject Extraction	Who do you think likes John?	Who do you think that likes John?
Object Extraction	Who do you think John likes?	Who do you think that John likes?

NOTE: Each dimension of the table represents a "factor" of the design. Thus there is a "that" factor (Presence/Absence of "that") and an Extraction Site factor. Each factor in this design is said to have two "levels" (e.g., Subject Extraction and Object Extraction are each levels of the Extraction site factor. This is said to be a 2 × 2 design because it has two levels on each of two factors.

experimental ideal would be to take "Who do you think likes John?" and make it into a "that"-trace violation without changing its surface form at all. That of course can't happen, but by adding "that" to the sentence, the interpretation of any observed difference in acceptability between the forms of this sentence with and without "that" becomes more difficult. The fact that the sentence becomes a word longer, that the added word is of unknown relevance to many of the confounding factors listed above, that the clausal structure of the sentence is somehow highlighted by the added word, and so on, all raise legitimate questions about how any observed difference in acceptability is to be interpreted. Factorial designs control for this kind of confounding by effecting the very same sort of manipulation in another set of very closely parallel conditions. Thus, instead of inserting "that" only into a subject extraction case, it is also inserted into an object extraction case. Because this is apparently immune to the "that"-trace effect, it can serve as a control case. Now the "that"-trace effect is, strictly, the difference between two differences: the difference between subject extraction sentences with and without "that," and the parallel contrast in object extraction sentences. The "that"-trace effect is now seen as a greater decrement in acceptability when "that" is added to subject extraction cases than occurs when "that" is added to object extraction cases.

Another useful way of looking at the type of structure shown in Table 2 is that it isolates two factors, Extraction Site and the Presence or Absence of "that," and sets up an interaction between them. Structuring materials in terms of factorial patterns makes it possible to use some of the more powerful statistical tools available.

Table 3 A factorial presentation of a coordination paradigm.

	Antecedent Location	
	Local Antecedent	*Remote Antecedent*
Coordination Type		
No Coordination	Cathy's parents require that Paul support himself.	Paul requires that Cathy's parents support himself.
Simple Coordination	Cathy's parents require that Paul support himself and the child.	Paul requires that Cathy's parents support himself and the child.
Coordination with "both"	Cathy's parents require that Paul support both himself and the child.	Paul requires that Cathy's parents support both himself and the child.

NOTE: There are two factors, Antecedent Location and Coordination Type, with two levels of the first of these and three levels of the second. Thus this is described as a 2 × 3 design.

Another illustration of a factorially structured set of materials comes from the coordination experiment discussed in Section 1.3.3 (see Table 3). Here, one of the two intersecting factors, the Coordination Type factor, has three "levels." Indeed, factorial designs may have, in principle, any number of different factors and each factor can have any number of levels. However, practical and interpretable experiments will usually have only very modest numbers of factors and levels of those factors.

The main virtue of designing materials in terms of factorial structures is that it facilitates distributing extraneous systematic factors uniformly across the experimental conditions. In paradigms such as those shown above, whatever effects are peculiar to the particular lexical items and grammatical structures used in any one sentence are likely to appear in all the others as well.

Unfortunately, the formal symmetry of a well-designed token set cannot ensure the relevant sort of linguistic uniformity across all the sentences within that token set. Formally driven variations in the specific form of some base sentence type can sometimes produce surprising interactions where one or more sentences in the set become strange in a way unlike parallel cases in other token sets. If properly controlled, such interactions can be a research topic. If not controlled, they confound and can completely undermine particular experiments.

In a typical psychophysical experiment that was intended to compare six very similar stimuli (as in Table 3), all six stimuli would probably be presented to each informant (possibly many times each). There are, however, further constraints that are usually applied in experimental work on sentence materials; no more than one member of a token set such as in Table 3 is presented to any one informant, and each sentence an informant judges is seen only once. The single presentation constraint is motivated by the assumption discussed earlier that sentences change informants. By hypothesis, the informant is never able to confront a sentence in quite the same way twice. Any future encounter with the same sentence is likely to be influenced in some way by the prior encounter. (See Note 4, Chapter 1, p. 29, this volume.) The one-sentence-per-token-set constraint is similarly founded. There is experimental evidence (Bransford & Franks, 1971) indicating that presentations of different but related sentences within an apparently random list of sentences can nevertheless be integrated by informants. Thus again the processing of the second sentence seems likely to be affected in some way by the informant's prior encounter with a related sentence. In effect, the constraints against repeated presentations or multiple presentations from a single token set are aimed at making each encounter between informant and sentence as much like a natural informative encounter as possible. The mechanics of constructing sentence lists that respect these constraints are discussed in Section 9.5.1.

Finding Verbs

Fleshing out an experiment design is mostly a matter of building a list of token sets that correctly implement the design without inadvertently introducing extraneous systematic variance of some kind. In many cases, the core of this process consists in finding a set of verbs appropriate to the needed structures. Indeed, it is often wise to develop, carefully evaluate, and filter a list of verbs before constructing any actual sentences.

The best aid in this process is the experience of an investigator who is very well versed in the issue at hand. Syntacticians can sometimes readily generate lists of verbs that exhibit specific properties.

Where more formal searches are undertaken, dictionaries that include explicit grammatical tags (if they are sufficiently detailed) may be helpful. Often, however, dictionaries generate lists of candidates that include many items that are irrelevant to a particular search, making the process of identifying the target items quite tedious. A shortcut that sometimes facilitates this sort of search can be done with a thesaurus. The investigator begins by building the largest possible set of appropriate candidates from memory or experience and then looks each of these up in a thesaurus (electronic ones are handy for this purpose). Generally the verbs linked to the those in the initial list will include some with similar syntactic properties. This process can then be repeated for all new items found.

3.4 Controlling Context

There is evidence that the context in which sentences are judged (i.e., other sentences seen previously) can affect judgments. Two elements of the experiment designs used in the work reported in Chapter 1 are intended to manage context effects.

Order of presentation clearly affects sentence responses. Indeed, some lines of psycholinguistic investigation have been built on exactly the influence that a preceding sentence can exert on the syntactic processing of a following sentence (see Bock, 1987, 1990). Thus the procedures to be described below will present any one list of materials in at least two different orders to efface order effects as much as possible. This of course does not eliminate order effects. Rather, it merely distributes them across the various experimental conditions in such a way that they are unlikely to systematically distort effects attributable to the targeted differences among sentence types.

Filler sentences, which made up the majority of the sentences informants judged in all of the experiments described in Chapter 1, play several important roles in a judgment experiment. They create the linguistic background against which the experimental sentences are judged and at the same time provide a kind of global anchor that can strongly affect both the overall range of responses given to the experimental sentences and the location of that range relative to the mean of all the responses in a session. Filler sentences, when well chosen, can provide a kind of benchmark against which experimental results from different experiments can become comparable. Fillers also disguise the pattern of the experimental items, making it harder for informants to guess which kinds of sentence the experimenter is interested in. This can be important because when informants are able to detect repeating patterns in the materials or other aspects of the experiment, there is a danger that they will adopt response strategies that are unrepresentative of their general behavior. Finally, filler sentences can also serve to qualify informants by allowing the experimenter to determine whether the informant is behaving "normally" without reference to the experimental materials. For example, sometimes in a session an informant will invert the response scale, using the high end to represent sentences of low acceptability and vice versa. Such cases are easy to detect with appropriate analyses on fillers.

Because fillers create the general background against which the experimental sentences are judged, they can have a marked effect on the average rating given to experimental sentences. Cowart (1994) shows that using a mixed filler list (two thirds highly acceptable sentences, one third sentences of very low acceptability) as opposed to a pure list (all highly acceptable) can shift overall ratings on experimentals up substantially (though without exerting any discernible influence on the overall pattern of response).

The best strategy is to include a balanced list of fillers that includes approximately equal numbers of sentences at a wide range of acceptability values.

3.4.1 Overview

In the approach described in this chapter, the core of a sound design for an experiment on sentence acceptability is a paradigmlike factorial structure that specifies and integrates one, two, or more syntactic variables whose effects on acceptability are to be tested. The heart of the process of executing an experiment designed along these lines consists in developing a list of token sets that accurately implement the intended syntactic contrasts without simultaneously inducing unwanted or uncontrolled differences among the experimental conditions. The background for the presentation of these experimental sentences is provided mostly by a set of filler sentences. By careful control of the distribution of experimental and filler sentences across lists to be judged by various groups of informants, and by appropriately varying the order in which materials are presented, it is possible to construct experiments that reliably detect a wide range of syntactically interesting differences in the relative acceptability of various sentence types.

All of the designs discussed so far have been what are called "within subject" designs. That is, they are intended to detect differences across sentence types by assessing each informant's average response in each of several sentence type categories. By augmenting a within subjects design with a between groups factor that distinguishes in some fashion among different types of informants, designs of this kind can be extended to address many sorts of differences among groups.

Note

1. This gem of unprocessable English is due to Raymond Smullyan.

4

The Sentence
Judgment Task

At various times, investigators have sought judgments on acceptability, on acceptability relative to some context, on grammaticality,
on possibility or plausibility assuming some referential interpretation, on truth relative to a picture, and on a variety of other aspects
of speaker responses to sentences. Although the relevance and interest of these various kinds of judgments is clear, the ability of informants to differentiate these types has not been carefully investigated.

   Most of the issues of experiment design that are discussed
elsewhere in this book are not very sensitive to the kind of question
put to the informant. Most of the general principles relevant to the
design of materials and the overall organization of an experiment
would apply to experiments on, say, judgments relative to scope
possibilities or possible patterns of reference relations, but I will
elsewhere assume that the target is a global judgment of the acceptability of each sentence in isolation. This sort of judgment seems to

reflect the operation of powerful and orderly aspects of the cognitive system of language, and thus is often seen as centrally important to linguistic theory. In this chapter, however, I will briefly consider some of the issues that arise when informants are asked for different sorts of judgments.

The purpose of this chapter is simply to point out that the effects that an experimenter's instructions have on an informant's performance can never be assumed. Although there is good reason to explore effects associated with differing forms of judgment tasks, it will take a good deal of work to make the contrast between different sorts of tasks useful. I will illustrate this claim with a brief review of an experiment that was designed to test naive informants' ability to control the criteria they apply in forming judgments. Although the result is hardly definitive, it suggests something of the kind of work that is required to make alternative judgment tasks useful.

One of the concerns most commonly expressed about the use of naive informants is that it is thought to be difficult to provide informants with instructions that reliably elicit the "right" sort of judgments, that is, ones uncontaminated by extralinguistic concerns (see Bley-Vroman, Felix, & Ioup, 1988; Carden, 1970; Newmeyer, 1983, p. 61, among others). The experiments described in Chapter 1 generally ignored this issue; they used instructions that asked informants for very informal intuitive reactions to the sentences and specifically emphasized that informants were not to try to assess the sentences according to any grammatical rules they might have learned in school. This does not reflect a lack of concern for achieving uncontaminated results, but arises from the approach to this issue that is reflected throughout this book; here the emphasis is on experimental control rather than direct manipulation of the informant's approach to the task. Thus the intuitive instructions applied in most of the experiments described earlier should invoke a very inclusive criterion for judgment; the informant is invited to respond to each sentence on any grounds (other than school grammar) that seem appropriate to the informant.[1] The coordination experiment described in Section 1.3.3, however, divided informants into two groups, each of which was given one of the sets of instructions shown in Table 4. The "Intuitive Instructions" are representative of those used in most of the other experiments described in Chapter 1 while the "Prescriptive Instructions" were designed to invoke a prescriptivist stance toward presented sentences. This particular contrast was constructed be-

Table 4 Alternative instructions for a judgment experiment.

Intuitive Instructions

Please read each of the sentences listed below. For each sentence, we would like you to indicate your reaction to the sentence. Mark your response sheet A, B, C, or D. Use (A) for sentences that seem fully normal, and understandable to you. Use (D) for sentences that seem very odd, awkward, or difficult for you to understand. (Note: DO NOT USE "E.") If your feelings about the sentence are somewhere between these extremes, use one of the middle responses, B or C. THERE ARE NO "RIGHT" OR "WRONG" ANSWERS. Please base your responses solely on your gut reaction, not on rules you may have learned about what is "proper" or "correct" English.

Prescriptive Instructions

Please read each of the sentences listed below. For each sentence, we would like you to indicate whether or not you think the sentence is a well-formed, grammatical sentence of English. Suppose this sentence were included in a term paper submitted for a 400-level English course that is taken only by English majors; would you expect the professor to accept this sentence? Mark your response sheet A, B, C, or D. Use (A) for sentences that seem completely grammatical and well-formed. Use (D) for sentences that you are sure would not be regarded as grammatical English by any appropriately trained person. (Note: DO NOT USE "E.") If your judgment about the sentence is somewhere between these extremes, use one of the middle responses, B or C. Use B for sentences you think probably would be accepted but you are not completely sure. Use C for sentences you think probably would not be accepted.

---

cause various commentators suggested that the rather laissez-faire intuitive instructions we have generally used might suppress sensitivity to grammatical factors relevant to the coordination experiment described in Section 1.3.3.

For current purposes, the key question is whether informants actually use any different standards when they are asked to apply school grammar criteria in making sentence judgments. Note that the standard view seems to be that all of the Remote Antecedent sentences in (4) are unacceptable and presumably ungrammatical; it also provides no basis for differentiating these sentence types.

The result of this manipulation is displayed in Figure 11. The difference in instructions did not produce any difference of pattern that seems to matter to linguistic theory. Apparently, the same factors govern informant responses under both types of instructions.[2]

This result is not, of course, a definitive showing that instructions cannot affect informant responses, although it does corroborate

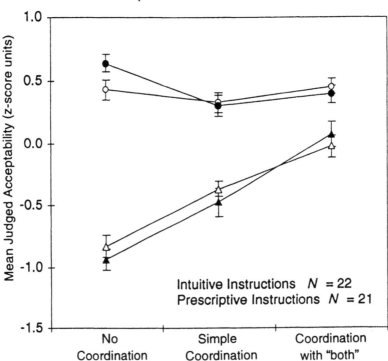

Figure 11. The interaction of coordination and binding effects under two different types of instructions to informants.

a general impression gained over many experiments that informants have very little ability to deliberately adjust the criteria they apply in giving judgments. Rather, the result serves primarily to emphasize that it is an empirical question whether any particular difference in instructions in fact affects informant responses, and, if there is such a difference, what form that difference takes. It seems plausible that instructions to informants to approach sentences in different ways can be used to highlight or emphasize different aspects of their overall response to sentences. The current result shows, however, that investigators who wish to ask informants to make different kinds of judgments will need to demonstrate two things. First, they will need to show that giving informants instructions other than those that ask for a global, intuitive assessment of the sentence produces consistent, systematic differences of pattern in informant responses.[3] Second, they will need to diagnose those differences that arise. That is, to make those differences of pattern fully useful, investigators will need to demonstrate that one sort of instruction makes informants comparatively more (or less) sensitive to specific aspects of the presented sentences (e.g., to processing difficulty associated with, say, rare vocabulary or known parsing complexity, or to semantic factors connected with reference or the empirical truth of the sentence). Insofar as these tests can be met, alternative instructions may be useful in exploring the cognitive resources that shape judgments.

An Aside on the Training of Linguists

In this context, it is perhaps appropriate to consider the commonplace suggestion that syntacticians in the course of their training gain insights into natural grammar that aid them in giving judgments uncontaminated by "extragrammatical" influences. This too is an empirical claim, but not one that has, so far as I am aware, been subjected to appropriate tests. There is nothing inherently wrong with the suggestion. There are many areas within medicine, the natural sciences, technology, and the arts where practitioners, after appropriate formal or informal training, become able to make sophisticated judgments about natural phenomena that cannot be replicated by untrained observers. Within linguistics, acquiring specialized skills of this sort is a standard part of training in some subdisciplines, such as phonetics. Nevertheless, in all the cases relevant to science, sophisticated observations can be checked against objective procedures. There are means by which the skills of individual investigators can be assessed by comparison to some observer-independent standard.

The same standards that apply to the assessment of procedures used with naive informants could apply to the training procedures to which linguists are subjected. If it is possible, for example, to train novice investigators to apply clear alternative criteria to judgments, it ought to be possible to demonstrate the effectiveness of these procedures. For example, a relevant experiment would subject a reasonably homogeneous group of graduate students to a single clearly specified course of study and training. At the end of this training, it ought to be possible to demonstrate that members of this cohort consistently differ from the general population in the pattern of response they produce with respect to numbers of syntactically relevant patterns. Furthermore, there ought to be at least as much consistency across individuals within this cohort as there is in the general population, and it should also be possible to demonstrate what specific factors the trained observers are more and less sensitive to relative to naive informants. There are a variety of obvious practical reasons why it would be difficult to organize and evaluate a training program along these lines.

The fact that no appropriately validated training program for syntactic informants is available makes data obtained from expert informants particularly difficult to interpret. Although there is little doubt that advanced training can lead to useful sophistication in the rendering of sentence judgments, there is no way to know how reliable current training regimens are nor any formal way to assess the skills of individual sophisticated informants. There is also good reason to believe that advanced training is at best a mixed benefit. Although it might be that sustained practice can sharpen an individual's ability to give reliable judgments, there are also reasons to suspect (as has often been suggested) that training can produce some theory-motivated bias. It is also worth considering that syntactic training leads to some amount of judgment learning; to read a syntax article intelligently usually requires that the reader hold in mind a particular pattern of judgments, whether or not those are the ones the reader finds most natural. Enough practice in this exercise could seriously distort an individual's ability to render the judgments that are most natural to his or her own grammar.

These considerations suggest that the relatively objective procedures described in this book (or other objective procedures) can play a useful role in providing relevant lines of evidence that do not rely on expert skills of unknown reliability.

Notes

1. It was thought appropriate to ask the informant to ignore school grammar precisely because this is an influence that seems to be something informants are

consciously aware of. Asking informants to make distinctions among syntactic, semantic, pragmatic, and other sorts of influences is quite another matter.

2. The interaction among the instructions variable, antecedent location, and coordination type did yield a small reliable difference, $F_1(2, 82) = 3.71^*$, $F_2(2, 46) = 4.18^*$. Note, however, that there appears to be no difference in pattern of any theoretical interest for the results obtained under the two sets of instructions.

3. Gross differences in overall acceptability will be relatively easy to obtain, but these are of no particular theoretical interest.

5

Presenting Sentence Materials to Informants

All of the experiments discussed in Chapter 1 used written presentations of sentence materials to informants. There is little doubt that judgments will differ for at least some classes of sentences if the sentences are presented to informants in some other way. There are, however, drawbacks associated with any choice of presentation method. Table 5 presents an overview of some advantages and disadvantages of various modes of presentation. Although this is hardly an exhaustive list of all the possible permutations, it may be useful in suggesting some of the considerations that ought to guide the choice of mode of presentation.

Interesting facets of the psycholinguistics of the judgment process may be revealed by manipulating mode of presentation, although

Table 5 Comparisons of alternative ways of presenting sentence materials to informants.

Presentation Mode	Advantages	Disadvantages
Written (printed questionnaires)	Easy to prepare and administer. Facilitates collecting data from large numbers of informants. Permits testing many informants simultaneously. Multiple versions of the question-naire can be presented simultaneously.	Relies on reading ability, which is both limited and variable in the general population. Speakers may have different expectations (or tolerances) for the syntax of written sentences than they do for spoken sentences.
Spoken (live presentation by experimenter)	Does not rely on literacy skills of the informant. Can be used to present materials to groups of informants simul-taneously. About as easy to prepare as written presentations.	Experimenter may inadvertently bias or influence the informant's responses. Testing groups of informants simultaneously is somewhat more awkward than with written presentations. Potential for different patterns of results from different experimenters. All informants present must respond to the same materials in the same order.
Recorded (computer or tape recording presented via loudspeaker)	Similar to above. More controllable and more consistent across multiple presentations of the same sentences (e.g., to different groups or individuals).	Time-consuming to prepare and execute. Somewhat cumbersome equipment may be required. All informants present must respond to the same materials in the same order.
Recorded (computer or tape, presented via headphones in laboratory setting)	Similar to above. Better control of experimental situation. Better opportunity to elicit full cooperation and effort of informant. Materials can be presented to each informant in a unique order.	Time-consuming to prepare. Relatively unnatural mode of interaction with informant. More labor-intensive per informant. Expensive and difficult to run more than one informant at once.
Synthesized speech (computer generated speech)	Similar to above. Potentially provides maximum control of stimulus. Potentially easier to prepare than recorded presentations.	Most readily available synthesis technologies produce poor quality speech. Tweaking improves result but at the cost of reducing the basic advantage of easy preparation. Unnatural mode of interaction in the informant session.

the constraints discussed in Chapter 4 will apply here as well; if systematic differences in patterns of response can be demonstrated for different presentation modes, it will be necessary to diagnose and identify those differences to exploit them effectively.

6

Response Methods
and Scaling Issues

The simplest method of collecting responses in informal syntactic research is an instance of a forced choice procedure—the informant is
given only "yes" and "no" as possible responses. Increasing awareness
of intermediate possibilities (in judgments and in the grammar) and the
frequent discomfort of informants faced with forced choices has led
many investigators to offer informants one or more "maybe" or other
intermediate responses between the extremes of the scale (see Schütze,
1996, pp. 44-48, for a review of current descriptive practice).

Investigators have sometimes been concerned to try to match
the array of responses they offer informants to the array of degrees
of grammaticality they posit in the grammar. This is less important
than sometimes supposed, as the discussion in Section 1.2 in Chapter
1 suggests. If the set of possible responses exceeds the number of
categories provided by the grammar, no information is lost by providing excess categories, and continued investigation ought to reveal

whether and how categories can be combined. Even at the opposite
extreme, if grammaticality is assumed to vary continuously, useful
data could still be collected via forced choice procedures. More
grammatical sentences will get a higher percentage of "yes" responses, and the frequency of "yes" responses should change continuously as grammaticality changes. This rather insensitive procedure will require larger numbers of informants to reliably detect
small differences in grammaticality, but there is no inherent limit in
the degree of detail it could detect.

When investigators offer informants an array of response options (even if there are only two), they are engaging in an exercise in
measurement; that is, they are attempting to assign labels or numbers
to a phenomenon according to a rule. In such circumstances, it
becomes important to attend to the properties the investigator and
informant are ascribing to those symbols or numbers that represent
the outcome of each judgment event.

An array of possible responses may be either ordered or unordered. A set of unordered responses might differentiate among
reasons for deviance, as in a set such as "OK," "Sounds incorrect,"
or "Hard to understand." In such a case, the analysis of the result will
proceed along quite different lines than the analyses of the sample
experiments discussed in Chapter 1. Here the investigator will need
to compare the percentage of responses in the various categories for
various items, but there will be no continuum that unites the categories. This is an instance of what statisticians term *nominal data* (see
Table 6); it consists in distributing a set of individuals, or a set of
responses, across a set of unordered, discrete categories.

In more typical judgment studies, the various response options
are seen as an ordered series of points on a scale. In this case, several
different mathematical interpretations of the relation between the
points on the scale are possible and the difference between interpretations may have important consequences for the interpretation of
scale values and for the choice of appropriate statistical tests.[1]

If the response options are merely ordered, the scale yields
what is known as "ordinal data"; here, if two sentences are found to
have different scale values, we can determine from those values
which sentence is the more acceptable, but nothing more. In particular, a difference in scale values on an ordinal scale carries no information about the size of the acceptability difference between sentences. To capture this further kind of information, the scale must

Table 6 Measurement scales.

Scale	Operations Performed	Permissible Transformations
Nominal	Identify and classify	Substitution of any number for any other number
Ordinal	Rank order	Any change that preserves order
Interval	Find distances or differences	Multiplication by a constant Addition of a constant
Ratio	Find ratios, fractions, or multiples	Multiplication by a constant

SOURCE: After Stevens (1975).

yield what is called "interval data." An interval scale carries information about the sizes of the differences between points on the scale. A 10°C range between daily high and low temperatures reflects the same size interval whether the day's high is 10°C or 20°C, but we cannot say (at least from a physicist's point of view) that a 20°C day is twice as warm as a 10°C day because this scale lacks a true zero point. When a phenomenon can be measured on an interval scale, a range of more powerful statistical tools becomes available for examining the resulting data. In the case of sentence acceptability, measuring on an interval scale makes it possible to determine which of two *differences* in acceptability is the larger one. A study that seeks to compare the impact of a subjacency violation and an ECP violation would need interval level data.

In principle, there is a still more informative interpretation that is sometimes available, but its relevance to the measurement of acceptability is uncertain. If a scale yields "ratio data," it becomes possible to calculate the relative sizes of individuals. That is, we can say of a cabbage that it weighs twice as much as another because this scale does have a true zero point. If in the linguistic domain a set of subjacency violations and a set of ECP violations could be measured on a ratio scale, we might be able to describe the results in terms such as these: Subjacency violations are, on average, twice as acceptable as ECP violations, or 33% more acceptable, and so on. Whether a ratio scale for measuring acceptability can be constructed is quite unclear at present. See the references in Endnote 1 in this chapter and Bard, Robertson, and Sorace (1996) for further discussion of issues in scaling.

The problem of measuring acceptability is the problem of constructing a response mechanism for informants to use that will reliably deliver interval level data. I will assume that the human cognitive system constructs judgments in such a way that there is in principle a relatively smooth and continuous interval scale of acceptability along which the acceptability values of all sentences lie. It does not follow from this assumption that any particular response scale will actually produce interval level data. Even when an investigator conceives of a set of response options as an interval scale and instructs informants to use it accordingly, merely ordinal data may result. The balance of this chapter is concerned with this issue.

6.1 Category Scale Methods

A category scale is simply a sequence of response categories that are understood to be uniformly spaced along some underlying continuum. Thus we could construct category scales with two, five, twenty, or more discrete steps that would evenly divide up the perceived continua of pitch, loudness, or other perceptual phenomena.

Category scales have been in use for a very long time[2] and they continue to be of value. Indeed, all of the experiments described in Section 1.3 used category scales. Category scales are attractive because they are conceptually simple, easy to explain to informants, and quick and easy for informants to use. They also produce data that are relatively easy to collect and to process.

Unfortunately, when linguists have constructed scales on which to rate sentences, they have not always attended carefully to the distinction between ordinal and interval scales. Occasionally an investigator will clearly intend that a series of response categories be seen and used as a scale, and yet, in addition to describing the extremes or the scale as a whole, will also attempt to describe the inner categories. The scale given in Table 7 illustrates this approach.

Even without the associated numerical labels, most informants could tell from these descriptions which of two response categories is meant to be the better one. It is very difficult, however, to ensure that informants will interpret the descriptions of the intermediate categories such that all adjacent pairs of values represent the same sized difference in acceptability. Attempts to explicitly describe the inner scale values are probably as likely to defeat uniform treatment

Table 7 Caricature of an ill-advised technique for constructing a category scale.

Rating	Description
1	Entirely natural and acceptable
2	Acceptable, but possibly a little unnatural
3	Doubtful, although possibly acceptable
4	Worse, but not entirely unacceptable
5	Completely unnatural
6	Terrible

Table 8 A definition of a five-point category scale.

... Mark your response sheet A, B, C, D, or E. Use "A" for sentences that seem fully normal, and understandable to you. Use "E" for sentences that seem very odd, awkward, or difficult for you to understand. If your feelings about the sentence are somewhere between these extremes, use whichever one of the middle responses seems most appropriate. ...

of the scale as to facilitate it. If informants don't manage to construct approximately equal intervals between the units of the scale, rating responses may not meet the mathematical assumptions of statistical tests such as t-tests and ANOVAs.

It is generally wiser simply to identify a scale for the informant, and perhaps to describe its end points, without attempting to describe any intermediate scale values. Table 8 illustrates this approach.

This scale description is meant to invite uniform treatment of the intervals without explicitly discussing the relation between different scale categories.

Unfortunately, the intended relation between the steps of a category scale can be difficult to obtain in practice. Stevens and Galanter (1957) demonstrated that when category scales are applied to a variety of continuously varying phenomena, subjects often use these scales as though there were systematically different sized intervals between steps of the scale. This is especially true when the stimuli to be judged are distributed unevenly across the scale. Gescheider (1976, p. 108) suggests one possible cause of this difficulty is that subjects usually feel pressed to try to use the full scale for whatever stimuli are presented and will try when possible to use all categories about equally frequently. Although distortions due to these problems are not necessarily dramatic, these considerations do suggest caution when investigators are considering the use of a category scale.

In general, it seems wisest to strive for the highest level of measurement that seems theoretically appropriate to the phenomenon in question. This gives the best prospects for the reliability of statistical results and provides the richest description of the phenomenon. Nevertheless, there may be circumstances where the simplicity and economy of the category scale will outweigh the risk that it will fail to yield interval level data. Some theoretical questions are resolvable by evidence that merely determines whether two sentences types have the same or different degrees of acceptability (i.e., where ordinal results are sufficient). Even where the magnitudes of differences are crucial, category scales can yield interval level results if they are used with appropriate caution. The most important step to take in preparing an experiment that will attempt to derive interval scale data from a category scale procedure is to pretest and carefully evaluate all the materials to be presented to informants. The goal here is to ensure that the materials are more or less uniformly distributed over the range of acceptability values that the experiment will tap, without any noticeable preponderance of relatively very good or very bad sentences. If, for example, the ratio of target sentences to fillers is kept low and the fillers are distributed uniformly over a wide range of acceptability values, it seems likely that interval level measurement can be achieved for the target sentences. Also, although there are no practical statistical tools for correcting data from a category scale that has produced ordinal data, we'll see in Chapter 12 that there are statistical ways to ensure that no inappropriate conclusions are drawn from such data.

6.2 Ratio Scale Methods

Psychophysicists originally devised ratio scale procedures not only in the hope of providing more accurate scaling results but also in response to this discipline's long-held interest in locating the thresholds of various perceptual continua. Although the notion of a threshold of acceptability is of doubtful relevance to the study of language, ratio scale procedures provide the best prospects for achieving reliable interval level measurement of judgments of acceptability.

Stevens (1975) describes a variety of psychophysical applications of ratio scaling procedures and Bard et al. (1996) discuss the application of ratio scaling methods (especially magnitude estimation) to acceptability judgments.

Ratio scaling methods have been shown to provide a better alignment between scaled responses and a variety of physical continua than typically arise with category scale procedures (Stevens & Galanter, 1957). In general, ratio scaling methods are characterized by an effort to give the subject maximum freedom to set the magnitude and range of the responses. If, for example, the subject is asked to gauge the relative brightness of flashes of light, one possible response method would be for the subject to draw a line for each flash of light. The subject's goal is to make the ratios of the line lengths correspond to the brightness ratios of the flashes of light. In doing this, the subject is free to make lines of any length (within a predefined space) so long as the correct ratios are maintained. There are a great many response measures of this general type and they are widely used in psychophysics.

Although the analysis of ratio scale results is somewhat more labor-intensive than the analysis of category scale results, the extra effort is manageable for smaller studies (those that collect, say, 100 or fewer responses from each informant and use perhaps one to two dozen informants). For larger studies, however, the extra effort required to use ratio scale procedures can be quite burdensome. Thus this section will describe two standard ratio scale procedures (magnitude estimation and line drawing) as well as further variants of these methods that have been specifically adapted for use in large studies.

6.2.1 Magnitude Estimation

Magnitude estimation is one of the most commonly used methods of collecting responses in ratio scale procedures. In magnitude estimation, informants are told to represent their evaluation of each stimulus by assigning it a number. The number the informant chooses can be as large or small as he or she likes. It may be any real number or fraction, so long as it is not negative. The informant's choice of number is constrained only in this way: The proportional relation among the numbers assigned to different stimuli should reflect the proportions of the stimuli themselves; thus a sentence that is judged twice as good as another should get a number twice as high as that assigned to the other sentence (Baird & Noma, 1978; Gescheider, 1976; Lodge, 1981; Stevens, 1975).

Bard et al. (1996) report on an extensive series of tests with magnitude estimation and other ratio scale procedures that provide compelling evidence of the utility of these procedures for judging acceptability. Although most informants will not have encountered this procedure before, they seem to learn to use it rapidly and reliably.

The principal drawback to using magnitude estimation is that (although it has been shown to be very widely applicable) it requires a very modest degree of mathematical sophistication on the part of the informant. Not all informants are equally comfortable with numbers and it may be that some adult informants do not have sufficient facility with numbers to use magnitude estimation. Particularly where informants are very young, infirm, or illiterate, magnitude estimation may not be appropriate.

6.2.2 Line Drawing

Line drawing as a response is attractive because it demands nothing of the informant's numerical sophistication and relies instead on the ability to recognize proportions among lines. Line drawing responses are constructed by informants drawing lines in clearly defined spaces to represent the relative acceptability of a sentence. Results obtained with line drawing procedures align very closely with those obtained with magnitude estimation (Bard et al., 1996).

6.2.3 Scannable Line Drawing

A major limitation of magnitude estimation and line drawing methods is that coding data obtained via these methods is relatively time-consuming and somewhat error-prone. In magnitude estimation, each numerical response must be read and keyed into a computer file. With line drawing, each line response must be measured by hand.

We have devised several scannable line drawing procedures in our laboratory in an attempt to combine the convenience and economy of machine-scored response forms with the effectiveness and simplicity of line drawing in obtaining reliable interval level data.

Our procedures use a form that provides a ten-point scale for each response item. We instruct informants that they should regard the ten-point scale as a line (see the sample questionnaire in Appendix E). By selecting one of the ten items on the scale, they were marking the *end point* of a line. Although they are marking only the end point of the line, informants are told that they should use long lines to represent high acceptability and shorter lines to represent lower acceptability. Crucially, informants are free to set the range of those variations in any way they like. They can, for example, vary their responses between the second and fourth points on the scale, or between the first and tenth. Their goal is simply to use line lengths represented in this way to accurately indicate the relative acceptability of the sentences presented to them. We find that informants readily grasp the instructions for using this method. By incorporating some elementary psychophysical scaling tasks within various experiments, we have demonstrated that informants use this method quite effectively and accurately to represent perceived magnitudes.

As a test of the effectiveness of our scannable line drawing procedure, we conducted parallel experiments, one using a magnitude estimation procedure and the other using a scannable ratio scale response. The results are summarized in Figure 12. The results from the two procedures were reliably similar ($p < .001$), with the magnitude estimation results accounting for about 85% of the variance in the scannable ratio scale responses.

Appendix E presents a set of sample instructions for a scannable line drawing procedure. The principal disadvantages of this procedure are that it takes more time to describe adequately for informants and, given its relative novelty, it requires greater caution in application. Until the procedure is applied more widely, it will be prudent for investigators to collect some data on a simple psychophysical task along with sentence judgment data to demonstrate the effectiveness of the procedure within each experiment. An example of a checking procedure appears at the top of the fourth page of the sample questionnaire shown in Appendix E.

6.2.4 Laboratory Implementations

When ratio scale methods are used in a laboratory setting, it becomes possible to use a variety of response mechanisms that are

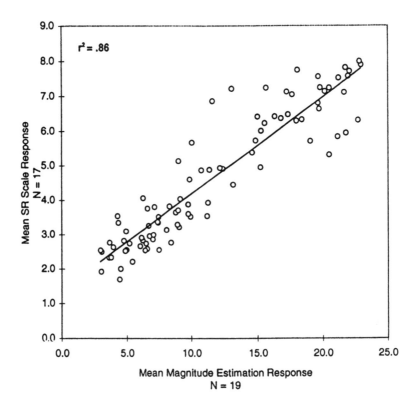

Figure 12. Results from a scannable ratio scale (SR) procedure compared with magnitude estimation.

NOTE: The graph compares the geometric means of scale responses from the nonstandard procedures to results obtained with magnitude estimation on the same sentences. The target sentences were 90 filler sentences that provided the context for a pair of "that"-trace experiments, each of which used a different scaling procedure. The number of informants who used each scaling procedure is shown in the axis labels for each graph.

easier to explain to informants and more natural than scannable line drawings. Informants can set the positions of dials that control sounds or lights (e.g., louder/brighter indicates higher acceptability), press triggers (higher pressure indicates higher acceptability), or set sliders on mechanical scalelike devices. Because of their simplicity from the informant's point of view, these response procedures will be attractive when they can be conveniently applied.

Overview

One central fact about human judgments about sentences seems to be that these phenomena are very richly structured. There appear to be subtle but stable differences among judgments people give across the whole range of sentences in a language. The problems of measurement considered in this chapter are the problems of capturing reliable information about those phenomena. The techniques and procedures discussed above seem to hold out the hope that linguists can capture a great deal more information about judgment phenomena than they have to date. Given the insights that have been uncovered via informally gathered judgment results, there is reason to hope that having more detailed and more reliable information about this phenomenon can help to uncover significant further insights.

Notes

1. There has been extensive discussion in the psychophysics literature on the question of which statistics are and are not appropriate with the various levels of measurement. Standard sources include Stevens (1975), Marks (1974), Baird and Noma (1978), and Gescheider (1976). A useful collection of papers debating questions about the propriety of using various statistical tests with various kinds of data appears in Kirk (1972, pp. 47-80).

2. Gescheider (1976, p. 110) reports on a scale astronomers used successfully for centuries to gauge the brightness of stars.

7

Sampling

The experiments described in this book are attempts to estimate the properties of a population on the strength of data collected from a sample drawn from that population. The relevant population might be the speakers of contemporary American English, the speakers of a particular midwestern variety of contemporary English, elderly English speakers in the Northeast, and so on. The population of speakers is always finite at the moment the sample is drawn, but open and able to include new speakers indefinitely (at least in principle). Obviously, the reliability of any estimate based on a sample is sensitive to the representativeness of that sample.

7.1 Representativeness

There are many familiar domains within the social and behavioral sciences where exacting control of the sampling process is critical to the representativeness of the sample. Polling on political and social issues is perhaps the most familiar example. Here very carefully drawn samples of 1,000 or more individuals are common. In general, the sampling process is critical whenever "typical" individuals are (or may be) unrepresentative of the population as a whole, or where the investigator intends to estimate the proportion of infrequent types of individuals (e.g., generally healthy 35-year-old males who show signs of subclinical aphasia). Statistical theory also leads to a concern with sampling because most statistical tests are based on a model that assumes random sampling from the relevant population.

This is not to say, however, that sampling is always a critical issue. Many samples used in biological, medical, and psychological research are controlled more by issues of convenience and economy than by sampling theory, and this does not generally reflect undue laxity on the part of the researchers who use these samples (although it can). Many biological phenomena are sufficiently consistent across individuals within a population to make drawing importantly un-representative samples far harder than drawing representative ones. For example, the relative length of the bones of the human upper arm and upper leg is quite consistent across individuals (though, of course, not invariant). Almost any small, casually drawn sample from individuals found in a school, hospital, jail, or shopping mall will provide an estimate of this ratio that will clearly distinguish humans from chimps or other primates. Countless other anatomical, physiological, and even behavioral traits show similar consistency across individuals in numerous species.

Notable consistency is also apparent in a variety of human behavioral traits, especially in language. Small samples are accepted for a wide variety of articulatory, acoustical, and perceptual studies of speech because theoretically relevant patterns can be readily and reliably detected in these small samples.

Thus the task of drawing a representative sample is not neces-sarily difficult. The degree of care appropriate to a particular experi-ment depends upon what is already known about the variability of the phenomenon in question (relative to the theoretically important contrasts to be tested) and what particular purposes the investigator has in mind. A medical researcher looking for reliable diagnostic signs of some disorder may need much more precise information about variation in contemporary human facial or body proportions than does a paleoanthropologist who is considering how to classify a particular fossil.

Experience to date suggests that language researchers who are working on widely spoken languages can select sufficiently representative samples in a wide variety of settings where a general mix of members of the target community are present. In the United States, these might include many schools and colleges, businesses, public offices, and similar sites so long as there is no reason to suppose that the particular site or institution might in some way attract (or repel) individuals according to what (syntactic) dialect they use. Because syntactic variation of the sort that generally interests syntacticians is so far from consciousness for most individuals, it is hard to imagine how any public institution could draw together an unrepresentative sample of speakers.

7.2 Linguist Informants

Perhaps the only class of sites that ought to be avoided in selecting samples for experiments on sentence judgments are those that have a high concentration of self-conscious language specialists (linguists, writers, editors, language teachers, and so on). It is entirely possible that among these groups, investigators can find the most skilled individual informants—those who can render quick, confident, and consistent judgments on their native language. Although these individuals may be extremely useful in exploratory research where the aim is to cover many phenomena quickly, or where the needed judgments require a sophisticated ability to focus on certain issues and ignore others, the representativeness of an individual informant can be established only through rigorous comparisons to larger samples.

7.3 Sample Size

The evidence reviewed in Chapter 1 demonstrates that judgments of acceptability, when collected via appropriate methods, are highly stable. Nevertheless, the evidence of error variance in judgments reviewed in Chapter 2 shows that several judgment phenomena in English are clearly not so stable that the responses of a single informant can reliably represent an entire community. Thus the practical question about sampling is this: How many informants is enough?

An important limitation on the possible answers to this question arises from constraints of experimental design. For example, the need to counterbalance and the structure of the "that"-trace paradigm given in (6) above combine to require that the minimum experiment on this phenomenon will use four informants. It is much better, however, to use a design that provides two different orderings of each of the materials sets, for a total of eight informants in the minimum "that"-trace experiment. Beyond this number, the number of informants required is determined by the stability of the phenomenon itself. Some differences in acceptability are large, others small. The number of informants needed will be greatest for experiments targeted on the smallest differences. Thus, for a phenomenon like "that"-trace, there are three possible reasonable answers to the question of how many informants are needed for an experiment on acceptability: (a) four, (b) eight, or (c) some higher multiple of four.

The data from a further "that"-trace experiment can be used to clarify this issue. This experiment employed four different ratio scaling procedures, each on a different group of informants, and was designed as a test of differences among these procedures. There were 71 informants, all of whom were tested on six sentences in each of the four relevant sentence categories. Overall, the experiment produced essentially the same results as the experiment described in Figure 4 and no differences among the procedures emerged. Nevertheless, the results show that high overall stability is consistent with considerable diversity among individual informants. Among these 71 informants, about one in ten showed a reversal of the standard "that"-trace pattern; for these informants, Subject Extraction with "that" is the most *preferred* sentence type. About one in five informants showed either this reversal or some other pattern clearly different than the norm. For 16 of these 71 informants, some condition other than Subject Extraction over "that" was the least preferred sentence type.

The impact of this level of variability was examined via a simple resampling procedure[1] in which a series of 20 random samples of size four were drawn from the data from the 71 informants. Subject Extraction with "that" was the least preferred sentence type in 19 out of 20 of these samples, as in the overall result. However, the critical interaction between "that" and Extraction Site was significant ($p <$ .05) in only 5 of the 20 samples. Of these 20 four-informant samples, most would have failed to detect the "that"-trace phenomenon by standard statistical criteria.

The results of a similar resampling test with samples of size eight were different. Among these 20 samples, all showed Subject Extraction with "that" to be the least preferred of the four sentence types, and the critical interaction between "that" and Extraction Site was significant in 17 of the 20 samples. That is, all but three of these "experiments" would have successfully detected the "that"-trace phenomenon. In short, phenomena whose effects are comparable in magnitude and complexity to "that"-trace can be reasonably investigated with samples as small as eight with the procedures used here.

Further tests were performed by combining data from two subjacency studies (see Section 1.3.1) with data from a third experiment that used the same type of materials. Between the three experiments, there were 173 informants. An analysis of variance showed that there was no reliable difference in overall pattern among the three data sets. As before, 20 samples of four were randomly drawn from this set. The Control condition was given the highest rating among the four conditions in all of these 20 samples. The overall ANOVA was significant in 18 of 20 of these samples. However, the definiteness effect (i.e., the difference between the Indefinite, Definite, and Specified Subject cases) was significant in only 2 of 20 samples. It appears that the large difference between the Control condition and the three others can be reliably detected with samples as small as four, but that the definiteness effect requires a larger sample.

As before, samples of eight produced effects much more like the full experiments reported earlier. When 20 samples of size eight were drawn from the full pool of 173 informants, all 20 samples showed an overall main effect, and the three-way contrast among the Indefinite, Definite, and Specified Subject cases was significant in 13 of 20 of these samples. Thus most of these "experiments" would have detected the definiteness effect, although somewhat larger samples would do better.

More formal methods for determining needed sample sizes are available (Cohen, 1969). These methods are based on the concept of "power" (the likelihood that a test will detect a real difference of a given size) and they corroborate the general picture described above.[2]

The practical conclusion these findings support is quite clear. For acceptability phenomena of the magnitudes relevant to many contemporary issues in syntactic theory, the minimum reasonable experiment will use eight or more informants. Some phenomena can be detected with smaller samples, and some phenomena will require larger informant groups, but few phenomena of current interest can be adequately described with fewer than eight informants.

7.4 Comparing Groups

The discussion of sampling thus far has assumed that the goal of research is to characterize general properties of groups of informants. There are also linguistic issues that call for drawing samples from two or more groups with a view to comparing the groups. If the differences among the groups to be compared are relatively stark, the differences may be detected with samples of sizes similar to those discussed above. However, some differences between groups may be stable but quite small. Where small differences are involved, group comparisons may require samples many times larger than those used in the studies discussed above. The size of differences can be estimated through pilot testing and this information can be used in estimating needed sample size.

Notes

1. A resampling procedure is one where numbers of small samples are randomly drawn from a larger sample to test various properties of the larger sample.

2. The methods Cohen (1969) provides for paired t-tests (pp. 60-64) can be adapted to all of the contrasts discussed here. These methods suggest that the "that"-trace phenomenon can be detected (with an 80% chance of success) with a sample of ten. Using the same criterion, the largest effects described above (e.g., the difference between local and remote antecedents where there is no coordinate structure) can be detected with samples as small as four to six. The smallest effects (e.g., the pairwise contrast between definite *picture*-NP cases and specified subject cases) require samples larger than 40. As noted earlier, whatever sample sizes the calculations of power provide, practical answers will generally be rounded up to the next higher multiple of (about) four because of constraints deriving from experimental design issues.

8

Settings for Experiments

In experiments on judgments (as in many psychological experiments on humans), there is a paradoxical need to both standardize and customize the procedure. On one hand, the experimenter's goal is to get each informant to do the same task and to rely on the same suite of cognitive resources to execute that task. On the other hand, each informant is an individual who comes to the experiment with a unique worldview, self-concept, personality, and temperament as well as a certain range of intellectual competencies. The informant also comes with ideas, attitudes, and opinions about language and his or her degree of competency in language, the status of the informant's own dialect or ideolect, the nature of experiments, the goals and interests of experimenters, and a host of other issues. This stew of factors can yield a wide range of results. While some informants are bored, contemptuous, or even (on rare occasions) uncooperative, others are painfully anxious to please the experimenter or intensely fearful that the procedure will expose some embarrassing deficiency (that will perhaps be secretly recorded). Thus the paradox is that, to get informants to behave uniformly for the purposes of an experiment, it may be appropriate to treat each one very much as an individual, to find a way to engage each individual's interest, to calm each individual's fears and anxieties, and to overcome each individual's particular misconceptions of the task he or she is being asked to do.

Every experiment has to negotiate a balance between the standardization of materials and procedure required to meet scientific goals and the individual customization needed to elicit the relevant sort of uniformity in human performance.

The survey procedures with which this book is primarily concerned obviously emphasize standardization over customization. Although informants can raise questions or concerns that are not answered by the questionnaire with the experimenter, the questionnaire must nevertheless do most of the work of eliciting the right sort of performance from the informant. Survey procedures compensate for whatever added variability there is in performance by making it feasible to collect data from many more informants than it is feasible to test in more individualized procedures.

In situations where there is an opportunity to brief informants individually and allow them to work in relatively private settings, this level of customization is worthwhile.

8.1 Survey Experiments

Survey experiments are relatively easy to conduct in a variety of institutional settings. In campus settings, a pool of informants can be recruited in a variety of ways. Where the experiment is appropriate in some way to the subject matter of a course, an instructor can sometimes justify taking class time for experiment participation, especially if the experimenter will agree to debrief the group on the experiment after they participate. Students can be asked to volunteer in class settings and in a variety of other ways (i.e., bulletin board notices, ads in a campus paper, and so on).

Wherever possible, informants should be compensated for their effort. This may come in the form of money or course credit, where appropriate. Sometimes students are required to participate in one or more experiments in connection with a particular course.

Most public institutions that have substantial numbers of people present on a regular basis provide some mechanisms by which informants can be recruited.

When a group of informants is assembled, it is often wise for the experimenter to try to elicit the informants' support and cooperation via some brief introductory comments. Informants should be assured that the work they are contributing to is worthwhile and that their contribution is valuable. It is also important to ensure informants that their responses will not be used in any way outside of the experiment. Indeed, unless the nature of the experiment makes it necessary to collect identifying information from each informant (e.g., where each will participate twice and data from the two sessions must be matched up), it is wisest to ask informants not to write their name or other identifying information on the response forms and to reassure them that their responses are entirely anonymous.

The main hazard in briefing informants prior to their participation is that it is possible to inadvertently bias informants in some way relevant to the experiment. Experimenters need to exercise caution to avoid saying anything that might indicate to informants which particular kinds of sentences the experiment is focused on.

It is a minor precaution, but one worth taking, to scramble the sequence of questionnaire types in a controlled way before distributing them to a group of informants.

It is generally wise to distribute questionnaires in such a way that one of each of the available types is distributed before a second copy of any of the types is distributed, and to ensure that all types have been used twice before any is used a third time, and so on. This helps ensure that informants in various parts of a room, or that come in during different parts of the day, are equally represented among each of the informant groups.

Procedures should be designed to be done in a reasonable amount of time. Tired, overworked, or impatient informants generally will not produce as clean data as more fit informants.

After informants have participated in an experiment, it is often desirable to provide them with a debriefing report or some other brief discussion of the experiment and its background. This is particularly important in collegiate settings, although it is relevant elsewhere as well.

8.2 Laboratory Experiments

Generally speaking, when laboratory versions of judgment experiments are undertaken, the same underlying concerns arise. The comments above and the instructions to informants given in Appendix E should suffice as a guide to the organization of judgment experiments in laboratory settings. The main advantage of laboratory settings is that there is a greater opportunity to tailor the process to the needs of the individual informant. The informant has more opportunities to ask questions that may improve the quality of his or her performance. In laboratory settings, it is also generally possible to create a unique order of presentation of materials for every informant. If there is another component of the task that does not involve giving judgments, the experimenter has an opportunity to provide feedback to the informant in the course of the session. This can be helpful in eliciting good performance in a variety of timed psycholinguistic tasks. Needless to say, in any variety of judgment tasks, experimenters should assiduously avoid any hint of evaluating, critiquing, or judging the sentence judgments informants make.

Another advantage of laboratory experiments is that there is usually an opportunity to debrief informants after the experiment session proper. This is sometimes a rich source of guidance for improving the procedure and better understanding the informant's perspective on the task. A debriefing session should also offer the informant some information on the goals of the experiment. However, when numbers of informants are recruited from a single socially interconnected group (e.g., a college class), informants should be asked not to share or discuss information they gain in the debriefing session with other prospective informants who have not yet participated.

8.3 Field Settings

One of the handier features of survey experiments is that they seem to elicit useful results even in rather unfavorable settings. In at least one case, informants have been recruited to participate in a judgment experiment as they came through the checkout line at a university cafeteria (with quite satisfactory results). Investigators who need to recruit informants in some similar setting should let preliminary results guide them as to whether informants perform normally in a nonlab setting.

9

The Organization and Construction of Questionnaires

This chapter will be concerned with the organization of questionnaires in experiments that use written presentations of sentence materials. The most important component of a questionnaire is a clear and consistent set of instructions and, usually, some preparatory exercises. The unreachable, but approachable, goal is to ensure that every informant has the same clear understanding of what is wanted. Recall that any differences across informants as to how the informant construes or approaches the task will contribute to error variance in the experiment.

Although questionnaires can be used in various kinds of experiments, the discussion here will assume that the target experiment is one that will involve a relatively large number of informants, and may be run at several sites by several different individuals. This is a somewhat extreme case that puts maximum pressure on the questionnaire itself to brief informants accurately and consistently. The general principles at work here apply also to simpler, less demanding circumstances and to the other settings discussed in Chapter 8. (At several points, the discussion will reference an example questionnaire shown in Appendix E.)

The objective of this chapter is to give a general outline of the logic of questionnaire construction. The discussion through Section 9.5 will leave it to the reader's imagination to determine how the various principles and effects specified here might be achieved. The last section of the chapter gives a kind of schematic procedure for implementing the logic described earlier. This procedure might be executed by hand or by way of various kinds of computer software—from word processors and spreadsheets to database programs. Appendix C provides still more concrete directions on how to construct questionnaires in a specific spreadsheet program, Microsoft Excel.

9.1 General Instructions and Demographic Data

In addition to instructions on the judgment task, informants usually need some guidance on various general aspects of the experiment. Informants should know who is responsible for the experiment and whom they can contact for further information. There may be multiple forms, documents, or other materials that informants will need to be introduced to, or special instructions on returning the answer sheet, and so on.

For many syntactic investigations, there will be no need to collect demographic data. For studies of variation where such data are relevant, it is perhaps wisest to collect the data after informants undertake the judgment task.

9.2 Response Training and Practice

In experiments that use category scales, it generally will be sufficient simply to describe the scale and how it is to be used. Most people, especially those who are college age or younger, are quite familiar with such procedures. However, experiments that use any variety of ratio scaling procedures will need to provide careful instructions on the scaling procedure itself. Unless the experiment uses instructions that

Table 9 Sample instructions for informants giving sentence judgment criteria.

We need some information from you about your evaluation of some sentences we've listed below.

We would like you to imagine that your job is to teach English to speakers of other languages.

For each sentence listed below, we would like you to do the following. Please read the sentence, then ask yourself if the sentence seems English-sounding or not. Suppose one of your students were to use this sentence. If we ignore pronunciation, would the student sound like a native speaker? Or would the sentence seem strange or unnatural to a native speaker no matter how it was pronounced? Your task is to tell us how English-sounding each sentence is, using a scale.

have been used and tested previously, it will be prudent both to test the instructions directly on a few informants and to include some check on the effectiveness of the instructions within the experiment itself. One good way to help the informant master the task and also check on the effectiveness of the instructions, informant by informant, is to include practice cases such as those included on the fourth page of the sample questionnaire ("Practice" section) in Appendix E.

9.3 Judgment Criteria

Questionnaires must specify for informants what criteria they are to apply in judging sentences. As noted in Chapter 3, there is little direct evidence that informants can in fact exercise any very subtle control over the criteria they use in judging sentences. Nevertheless, there needs to be some consistent guidance that leads informants' attention to the perceived acceptability of the sentences.

The instructions shown in Table 9 (taken from the questionnaire in Appendix E) have proven effective in this role, but many alternatives are possible.

9.4 Practice and Benchmark Materials

Even with quite straightforward procedures (such as using a category scale), informants usually need a little practice before they begin judging the main sentence list. Failing to provide practice or warm-up materials introduces unnecessary noise (i.e., error variance) into results from the first few sentences on the main sentence list.

It is sometimes helpful to include in a questionnaire one or more blocks of "benchmark" sentences that are identical across all versions of the materials, that appear in the same linear position within the materials to be judged (e.g., at the beginning), and that appear in exactly the same order (within the list of benchmark sentences). These sentences provide a baseline by which some useful comparisons can be made across informants, and help to detect certain kinds of error. For example, occasional informants will invert a response scale, using the high end as the low end. If an informant's pattern on the benchmark sentences is strongly but negatively correlated with the average pattern on the benchmark sentences, a scale inversion may well have occurred. A block of benchmark sentences appearing just before the beginning of the main sentence list (i.e., the target sentences and fillers that are the focus of the experiment) can double as practice materials, although in this case it might be wise to ignore results of the first half dozen or so items in the analysis to allow for instability while the informant is becoming familiar with the task. The first 10 sentences in the questionnaire in Appendix E (Items 11-20) are benchmark sentences.

9.5 The Main Sentence List

As noted in Chapter 3, the fundamental unit of account in constructing materials for sentence experiments is the token set. The number of token sets required for a particular experiment will generally be a function of two values: the number of sentences in each token set, and the number of sentences of each sentence type to be presented to each informant. Thus an experiment that has four sentences in each token set and that will present six instances of each sentence type to each informant will need 24 token sets.

The experimenter will need to settle on some ratio of filler sentences to experimental sentences. In general, there should be at least twice as many filler sentences as there are experimentals; three to four times more fillers than experimentals is desirable where this does not lead to an unreasonably long questionnaire. If the ratio of

Table 10 Rules for counterbalancing the sentence lists presented to different groups of informants.

• Each informant will judge no more than one sentence from each token set.
• Each informant will judge all experimental conditions and will see equal numbers of sentences from each condition.
• Every sentence in every token set will be judged by some informant.

---

fillers to experimentals goes to two or below, there is an increasing danger that informants will become particularly aware of the sentence types the experiment features, with unpredictable consequences for the informants' patterns of response.

9.5.1 Counterbalancing

The goal of counterbalancing is to help efface the effects of factors irrelevant to a particular experiment and to highlight those effects the experiment is designed to reveal. As noted earlier, informant responses to sentences can be very sensitive to a wide variety of factors other than the logical and structural features of sentences that interest syntactic researchers. Nevertheless, structural features must always be implemented in specific sentences with specific lexical content. Thus any single global judgment about a particular sentence is necessarily suspect; there is no usable way to determine how various disparate factors contributed to its formation and thus no easy way to determine how that single judgment is relevant to the many theoretical questions to which the target sentence might be relevant. Counterbalancing aims to distribute both the idiosyncratic and the systematic structural effects that arise in a single sentence across the whole experiment in such a way that the systematic effects can be reliably discriminated from the background blur of idiosyncratic effects.

Implementation of counterbalancing consists in honoring three rules in the construction of a set of sentences that informants are to judge. To satisfy the rules, it is necessary to divide the available informants into "materials groups" (of roughly equal size), there being as many of these groups as there are different sentence types in each token set. All the members of each "materials group" will judge the same subset of the experimental materials. The counterbalancing rules are enumerated in Table 10.

The consequences of the rules listed in Table 10 for a complete list of sentences are illustrated in Figure 13. In each of the scripts, there are equal numbers of each sentence type.

9.5.2 Blocking

Note that counterbalancing has nothing to say about the order in which sentences appear. This leaves open the possibility (in fact, a likelihood) that a truly random procedure for ordering the sentences might concentrate all or most of the sentences of a given condition in one relatively small part of the list. This would be undesirable because the informant's state of mind may well change in relevant ways as she proceeds through the questionnaire. Fatigue, boredom, and response strategies the informant may develop over the course of the experiment can have differing effects on sentences judged at various points in the entire procedure. The role of blocking is to try to manage these unwanted effects by ensuring that they act on all experimental conditions equally.

In the standard case, there will be as many blocks in a sentence list as there are sentences of any given experimental condition in the list. We get the same result by dividing the total number of token sets by the number of conditions within each token set, because the total number of token sets should be an integral multiple of the number of conditions. In other words, if there are four sentence types represented in each token set, and if each informant is to judge, say, six instances of each of those types, the list of materials the informant will judge will be organized into six blocks.

To implement blocking, a controlled randomization procedure should assign each experimental sentence to a block so that only one sentence of each type appears in each block. Each block should also contain the number of filler sentences determined by the filler ratio; that is, we multiply the number of experimental sentences in the block by the ratio of fillers to experimental sentences to determine how many fillers should appear in each block. Figure 13 shows two example schematic scripts that have been organized by blocks that respect the principles stated above.

Materials

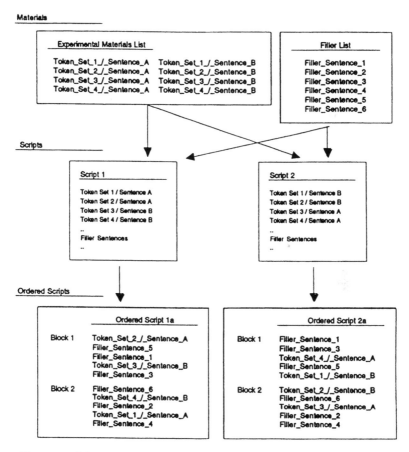

Figure 13. Schematic example of counterbalancing.

NOTE: This illustration shows how lists of token sets and fillers can be distributed across two scripts and two ordered scripts in a way that is consistent with the counterbalancing rules stated in Table 10. At the first stage, the Experimental Materials List is divided so that every sentence from every token set gets passed on to some script, and so that all the types of sentences (just two in this case) are equally represented in each script. When the resulting lists of experimental materials (what I sometimes refer to as preliminary scripts) are combined with the filler list (which is the same in both cases), the result is a script, a particular subset of all the sentences used in the experiment. To put the materials in each script into an order, it is necessary first to organize them into blocks with one experimental sentence of each type in each block and whatever number of fillers needed to fill out the block (there being the same number of fillers in all blocks). Both the assignment of the sentences in a script to blocks and the final ordering of materials within each block are randomly determined. Many different ordered scripts can be derived from any one script (hence the lowercase letters at the ends of the ordered script names). Where this is feasible (as in computerized laboratory experiments), each informant should see a unique ordered script.

9.5.3 Randomizing

Randomizing sentence lists is done within blocks. Generally, a truly random procedure within the block is appropriate. Occasionally, it may be appropriate to control the randomization procedure to ensure that experimental items don't appear within the first two or three items of the first block if there are to be particularly few warm-up or practice items.

9.5.4 Multiple Scripts and Versions of Scripts

There will be as many different scripts in an experiment as there are conditions within each token set; the number of sentence types per token set determines how many different materials groups will be needed to satisfy the counterbalancing rules. Each script should be constructed along the lines described above. The process that creates ordered scripts (both the assignment of experimentals to blocks and the randomization of order within blocks) is done independently for each script. Furthermore, because order (as noted earlier) can influence the results for individual sentences, it is highly desirable to construct two or more independent orderings of each script. Although this exercise may seem somewhat excessive (or obsessive), without this degree of caution, it is common to find unwanted and uninterpretable statistical interactions among the experimental factors and those factors that represent the assignment of informants to scripts or the assignment of token sets to conditions.

9.6 Constructing Questionnaires

This section will outline a process for constructing questionnaires. It will assume that the process is executed in spreadsheet and word processing software but will not be concerned with details of implementation. Those investigators who are sufficiently familiar with the relevant software tools will be able to carry out the process from the description provided here. Those who would like guidance on the use of the relevant functions in Excel will need to consult Appendix C.

Table 11 Experimental sentences projected from sentence components.

Sentence Components	Token Set 1	Token Set 2
Component A (main clause)	Who did the counselor want	Who would Nona like
Component B (complementizer)	for	for
Component C (subordinate clause, subject trace)	to hug Chantal?	to pay Sarah?
Component D (subordinate clause, object trace)	Chantal to hug?	Sarah to pay?
Sentences Projected From Components		
No "for," Subject Extraction case	Who did the counselor want to hug Chantal?	Who would Nona like to pay Sarah?
No "for," Object Extraction case	Who did the counselor want Chantal to hug?	Who would Nona like Sarah to pay?
With "for," Subject Extraction case	Who did the counselor want for to hug Chantal?	Who would Nona like for to pay Sarah?
with "for," Object Extraction case	Who did the counselor want for Chantal to hug?	Who would Nona like for Sarah to pay?

NOTE: Here the components of two token sets are enumerated in the upper panel of the table. In the lower panel, spreadsheet functions have been used to assemble the components into finished sentences of the intended types.

9.6.1 Constructing Experimental Materials Lists (Lists of Token Sets)

It is easy enough to prepare lists of token sets as simple lists or tables of sentences in a word processor. Taking this approach, however, creates ample opportunities for errors to arise. A better approach is to construct token sets as ordered sets of sentence components and then to assemble those components into finished sentences via some automatic process (e.g., the concatenation functions exploited in Appendix C, although there are many other possibilities). This makes it much easier to ensure that the structure of each token set is consistent with the overall plan. This procedure is illustrated in Table 11.

9.6.2 Constructing Filler Lists

No special procedures are required for generating filler sentences, although it may be necessary to identify and label fillers carefully, especially if the filler list is structured according to the level of acceptability of each sentence.

9.6.3 Integrating Materials and Fillers by Blocks

The heart of each questionnaire is the list of sentences informants will judge. There are three parts to the process of constructing this list. First, the order of the final list of token sets to be used in an experiment should be randomized to minimize the chance of inadvertent similarities among items clustering together in particular questionnaires. Identification labels should also be assigned to the items and preserved in all further processing up to the final questionnaire.

Second, a counterbalanced set of preliminary scripts must be derived from the list of token sets that make up the experimental materials. A preliminary script is just the list of experimental sentences that will ultimately go into one questionnaire. The various sentences that make up each token set are distributed across the complete set of preliminary scripts in a way that respects the counterbalancing rules. Note that in Table 12, each of the preliminary scripts includes three sentences of each of the four types that make up each token set. The number of preliminary scripts constructed for an experiment should equal the number of different sentences that make up each token set (or some integral multiple of this number).

Third, a four-step process is used to combine each preliminary script with the list of filler sentences. This process is illustrated in Table 13.

The process described in Table 13 is less burdensome than it might first appear. The spreadsheet implementation described in Appendix C requires less than 2 minutes to construct each new ordered script. In Table 13, the sentences are represented only by their identifiers. Each panel of the table includes the same materials; only the order changes from panel to panel. In Step 1, a preliminary script is copied into the middle column of a matrix that includes preexisting block identifiers in the first column. Random numbers are then generated in the third column. In Step 2, each sublist of items of the same type (e.g., all the TS*nc* items, or all the F(iller) items) is sorted according to the value of the random number assigned to each item. Because the column of Block IDs is not included in the sort, the

Table 12 Preliminary scripts.

Preliminary Script 1	Preliminary Script 2	Preliminary Script 3	Preliminary Script 4
NT/SE	*NT/OE*	*WT/SE*	*WT/OE*
Who are the students assuming helped Vicky with the taxes?	Who are the students assuming Vicky helped with the taxes?	Who are the students assuming that helped Vicky with the taxes?	What are the students assuming that Vicky helped with the taxes?
Who did Sally mean had seen her father in the backyard?	Who did Sally mean her father had seen in the backyard?	Who did Sally mean that had seen her father in the backyard?	Who did Sally mean that her father had seen in the backyard?
Who did Nona estimate outscored Sarah?	Who did Nona estimate Sarah outscored?	Who did Nona estimate that outscored Sarah?	Who did Nona estimate that Sarah outscored?
NT/OE	*WT/SE*	*WT/OE*	*NT/SE*
Who do they figure the professor will impress?	Who do they figure that will impress the professor?	Who do they figure that the professor will impress?	Who do they figure will impress the professor?
Who had the people heard they would be fighting for?	Who had the people heard that would be fighting for them?	Who had the people heard that they would be fighting for?	Who had the people heard would be fighting for them?
Who could Jeff remember Tiffany had written to?	Who could Jeff remember that had written to Tiffany?	Who could Jeff remember that Tiffany had written to?	Who could Jeff remember had written to Tiffany?
WT/SE	*WT/OE*	*NT/SE*	*NT/OE*
Who had he dreamed that would marry me?	Who had he dreamed that I would marry?	Who had he dreamed would marry me?	Who had he dreamed I would marry?
Who did they claim that beat up the burglar?	Who did they claim that the burglar beat up?	Who did they claim beat up the burglar?	Who did they claim the burglar beat up?
Who might Emily declare that had avoided Henry?	Who might Emily declare Henry had avoided?	Who might Emily declare had avoided Henry?	Who might Emily declare Henry had avoided?

(continued)

Table 12 Continued

Preliminary Script 1	Preliminary Script 2	Preliminary Script 3	Preliminary Script 4
WT/OE	NT/SE	NT/OE	WT/SE
Who did the broker state that the accountant would fire?	Who did the broker state would fire the accountant?	Who did the broker state the accountant would fire?	Who did the broker state that would fire the accountant?
Who were the children told that they would write to?	Who were the children told would write to them?	Who were the children told they would write to?	Who were the children told that would write to them?
Who did the counselor recall that Chantal had hugged?	Who did the counselor recall had hugged Chantal?	Who did the counselor recall Chantal had hugged?	Who did the counselor recall that had hugged Chantal?

NOTE: Each preliminary script constitutes a counterbalanced set of experimental sentences that would be appropriate for use in one questionnaire. Every version of every token set is used in some preliminary script, and within each preliminary script, every sentence type is equally represented. All the sentences on each row are members of the same token set. The labels above each block of three rows indicate the type of the sentences in that block for that column, such as NT/SE (No "that"/Subject Extraction) or WT/OE (With "that"/Object Extraction).

Table 13 A process for integrating and ordering experimental materials and fillers by blocks.

Step 1	Step 2	Step 3	Step 4
Source: A preliminary script plus the filler list and random numbers	Randomization within types randomly assigns sentences to blocks	Sorting by block segregates blocks	Randomization within blocks determines final order

Blk ID	Item ID	Random #	Blk ID	Item ID	Random #	Blk ID	Item ID	Random #	Blk ID	Item ID	Random #
1	TS1A	.568	1	TS2A	.158	1	TS2A	.158	1	F15	.026
2	TS2A	.158	2	TS1A	.568	1	TS4B	.772	1	TS8C	.090
3	TS3A	.683	3	TS3A	.683	1	TS8C	.090	1	TS2A	.158
1	TS4B	.772	1	TS4B	.772	1	TS12D	.538	1	F7	.256
2	TS5B	.820	2	TS5B	.820	1	F15	.026	1	F18	.314
3	TS6B	.856	3	TS6B	.856	1	F7	.256	1	F6	.481
1	TS7C	.392	1	TS8C	.090	1	F18	.314	1	TS12D	.538
2	TS8C	.090	2	TS7C	.392	1	F6	.481	1	F16	.623
3	TS9C	.517	3	TS9C	.517	1	F16	.623	1	TS4B	.772
1	TS10D	.713	1	TS12D	.538	1	F17	.788	1	F17	.788
2	TS11D	.677	2	TS11D	.677	2	TS1A	.568	2	F5	.198
3	TS12D	.538	3	TS10D	.713	2	TS5B	.820	2	F2	.295
1	F1	.626	1	F15	.026	2	TS7C	.392	2	F14	.335
2	F2	.295	2	F5	.198	2	TS11D	.677	2	TS7C	.392
3	F3	.637	3	F12	.247	2	F5	.198	2	F11	.482
1	F4	.440	1	F7	.256	2	F2	.295	2	TS1A	.568
2	F5	.198	2	F2	.295	2	F14	.335	2	F1	.626
3	F6	.481	3	F13	.305	2	F11	.482	2	TS11D	.677
1	F7	.256	1	F18	.314	2	F1	.626	2	TS5B	.820
2	F8	.954	2	F14	.335	2	F9	.911	2	F9	.911
3	F9	.911	3	F4	.440	3	TS3A	.683	3	F12	.247
1	F10	.562	1	F6	.481	3	TS6B	.856	3	F13	.305
2	F11	.482	2	F11	.482	3	TS9C	.517	3	F4	.440
3	F12	.247	3	F10	.562	3	TS10D	.713	3	TS9C	.517
1	F13	.305	1	F16	.623	3	F12	.247	3	F10	.562
2	F14	.335	2	F1	.626	3	F13	.305	3	F3	.637
3	F15	.026	3	F3	.637	3	F4	.440	3	TS3A	.683
1	F16	.623	1	F17	.788	3	F10	.562	3	TS10D	.713
2	F17	.788	2	F9	.911	3	F3	.637	3	TS6B	.856
3	F18	.314	3	F8	.954	3	F8	.954	3	F8	.954

NOTE: "Blk ID" is a block identifier that initially assigns each item to a block. "Item ID" identifies each item by type and version; "TS1A" is Token Set 1 in version A and "F7" is Filler Sentence 7. See text for further discussion. Note that in the third block constructed in Step 4, there are three experimental sentences appearing consecutively. Experimenters should control the randomization process to prevent such occurrences.

effect is sentences randomly assigned to blocks within each subtype of sentence. Step 3 sorts the entire list by Block ID, which groups together all the items that will appear in each block. Randomizing the sequence of items within each block in Step 4 distributes the experimental and filler items more or less uniformly through the block. I'll call the lists that emerge from Step 4 just "scripts." Note that by repeating Steps 2-4 for the same preliminary script, we can generate several differently ordered versions of the same script. It is prudent to use at least two different orderings of each script; using only a single ordering of a script can lead to unwanted ordering effects that may obscure the main experimental findings. This process must be applied to each of the preliminary scripts.

It is important to preserve the files generated in the course of constructing scripts because the Item IDs in these files will later be used to decode the data files emerging from the scanning or data entry process.

9.6.4 Assembling Questionnaires

The final step in the process of assembling a questionnaire combines a script with a master questionnaire file. The master questionnaire includes all the instructions for informants and other invariant material that will appear in every questionnaire. Appendix E includes a complete questionnaire. The master questionnaire can be constructed so that a script can be copied into a predetermined location in a copy of the file with sentences being numbered automatically. The number of questionnaires generated should be equal to at least twice the number of types per token set.

10

Coding and
Decoding the Data

The responses informants produce usually require several stages of processing before the results of an experiment can be summarized or analyzed statistically. These processes include scanning machine-readable forms, cleaning up the data that emerge from the scanning process, or (with nonscannable response materials) keying in data. As in the previous chapter, I will provide an outline of the process experimenters need to apply here, but discussion of the specifics of implementing these processes in software is reserved for the appendixes.

 The processes described at the beginning of this chapter are specific to experiments that use scannable response forms in survey-type experiments. However, these processes converge with those arising in other types of experiments at the point represented by Figure 18 below. From that point on, the processes described here will apply to any judgment experiment of broadly similar design.

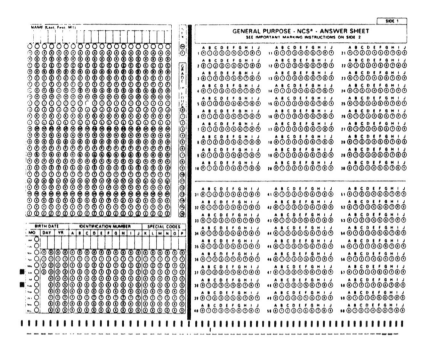

Figure 14. A standard NCS 10-alternative response form.

SOURCE: NCS General Purpose Answer Sheet, © National Computer Systems, Inc., Minneapolis, MN. Reprinted courtesy of NCS.

NOTE: The left-hand panel provides for various kinds of identifying information and demographic data. All of these fields can be adapted for special purposes. The right-hand panel includes 60 response items.

10.1 Scanning

It is often wise to review response forms before they are sent in for scanning. Occasionally, informants will make stray marks on their forms or mark their forms so carelessly that accurate scanning is unlikely. It can sometimes save later effort to darken light marks and erase stray marks at this stage.

Machine-readable response forms (see Figures 14 and 15) must be scanned by specialized equipment to extract numerical data. This service is available on most campuses and is also commercially available in many localities. University testing services that process machine-scored answer sheets for course tests can usually adapt their services for use in experimental work using machine-scored forms. There are standard ten-alternative and five-alternative versions of

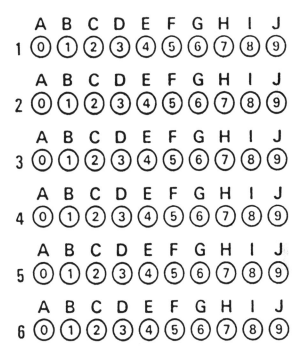

Figure 15. An expanded view of six response items from the form shown in Figure 14.

SOURCE: Form © National Computer Systems, Inc. Reprinted courtesy of NCS.

machine-scorable forms. Most campus testing services will have available software routines for analyzing test scores. Investigators will need to instruct the scanning service *not* to apply such analyses to data generated in experiments but to simply construct a results file that includes all the informant data. Usually result files can be returned to the investigator on a floppy disk or via e-mail.

10.2 Patching, Parsing, Decoding, and Sorting Scanned Data

Ideally, all the data from each informant will appear on one line (within one "record") in the resulting data file, and corresponding data items (e.g., the informant's response to the 25th sentence) will

Line 1	II	INSTRUCTOR A			
Line 2	II	F		055742162	172552367453559884995644996686649688 6
Line 3	II	G		070076478	029610390000996009800490994578135799 1
Line 4	II	F		088487455	190620796593293809098912908832872999
Line 5	II	H		031775095708862	07929526324726273928305738246761637 15
Line 6	II	B	RE	12 132645411	2 000077777777474335553225 62266077777 7
Line 7	II	E			09444158000002606000417211134305624 88
Line 8	II	A		103605967	05160079065139730847257644997966080 07
Line 9	II	G*** RLE DA NM RIE 0930740736891 57			2 040900490451539940944090944044404944 0
Line 10	II	BO ATO D Y X	100273056 58 7751		00111100010111000011110101100100110 101
Line 11	II	E		052564000	21690333893584566393549397893999793 4
Line 12	II	G		061702687	093944793894999944999796999999679999 7
Line 13	II	D		129727470	071400890190263019899999838024447920 95

Figure 16. Sample output from scanning.

fall in the same place (left to right) on each line, but this often is not the case. Scanning any more than a handful of forms seems almost always to result in at least a few anomalies (see Figure 16). For a variety of reasons, scanning systems often report blank data fields for unused fields and use long series of blanks as spacers in data files. This can make the process of interpreting a file of scanned data more challenging than it should be. Had the results represented by Figure 16 been ideal, the first 12 data lines (Lines 2-13) would all have been patterned exactly like Line 2. Note that over Lines 4 through 11, there are instances of missing data and spurious or surplus data (where informants appear to have filled in items they were asked to leave blank). Often scanned data look even less orderly on first appearance because they are organized into very long lines that break across two or three display lines in a word processor or editor.

Unfortunately, the only corrective for these sorts of anomalies is usually to edit the data file by hand. Many anomalies are obvious (e.g., excess data) but some will require reference to the original forms. It is generally easier to make the corrections with a word processor or text editor in the data file before it is processed further. It is also helpful in this process to use a monospace font (e.g., Courier).

In general, the goal at this stage is to have every line of the file conform to the same format, to ensure that the nth character on every line represents the same thing as the nth character on every other line (e.g., the third digit of the informant's ID number or the informant's 36th judgment response), to fill in any missing data that can be recovered via inspection of the original forms, and, above all, not to introduce any new errors via this editing process. The data file that results from this editing process should look something like the one shown in Figure 17. Once the file is in this form, it is ready to be moved into a spreadsheet for further analysis.[1]

INSTRUCTOR A

B	1345411	000077777777474335553225462266 0777777
F	0887455	1906207965939293809 0989129 08832872993
B	3058775	001111 00010111 00001111011100100110101
E	9999999	09444158000002606000417211134 38562488
G	0796478	02861 039000099960198049099457 81357991
A	1005967	05160079065139730847257644997966 08007
E	1281584	1 001100110100111111000100110100111100
H	0908862	07929526324726273928305738246 76163715
F	0542162	1 725523674535598849956449966866496886

INSTRUCTOR B

F	0988587	05230449216032796197117187027 43475852
E	0564000	19033389358456639354939978939 99793499
F	0683862	09831 088016040974 0994 094670761 0690790
G	0776478	02961 039000099960098049099457 81357991
F	0973127	1 011111011111100110110110010101011001
G	0602687	09394479389499994499979699999 96799997
D	1227470	0714008901902630198999998380 244792095
H	0742670	05372277565467584877776474757 77577777
F	1107405	07198039348071997099319889089 92697591

Figure 17. A cleaned data set.

When a data file of this sort is copied into a spreadsheet, all of
the characters in each line will generally be placed in a single cell (up
to the usual 256-character-per-cell limit). Thus the first spreadsheet
operation in an analysis is usually to parse the lines in the data so
that each "field" from the original appears in a separate cell of the
spreadsheet. That is, the series of digits that represent the informant's
ID (if any) should all be in the same cell of the spreadsheet, and each
single character that represents an informant response must be in a
separate cell. Some notes on the parsing process appear in Appendix
C. Figure 18 shows how the data should look after the parsing
process is complete. Note that each line now begins with a 1-charac-
ter field that indicates whether the informant was in the Instructor A
group or the Instructor B group.

Although the data are now orderly and consistent, they are not
ready for analysis because the informants represented in this table
(most of which is not visible) were using eight different questionnaires, as indicated by the second character in each row. The next step
toward getting the data in analyzable form is to sort the informants

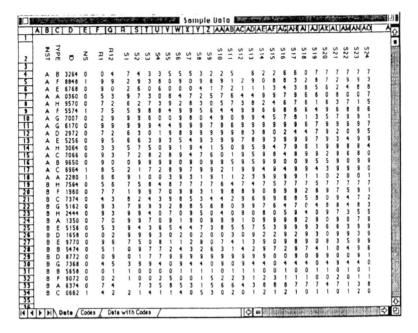

Figure 18. Parsed data in Excel spreadsheet.

NOTE: The data collected by Instructor A are now distinguished by a character code in the first column of the table. The TYPE column indicates which of eight different questionnaires each informant used and the ID column assigns a unique ID number to each informant. The fourth column, NS, is demographic data; 0 indicates that the informant is a native speaker of English. The next 12 items on each row represent the first 12 sentences the informant judged. These sentences were identical in content and order across all versions of this set of questionnaires. The columns containing data for sentences R2 through R11 have been hidden. The remaining 24 items on each line (S1-S24) represent both experimental and filler sentences in the linear order in which they appeared for each informant.

so that all those who used the same ordered script appear together in the table. Once the informants are grouped according to which ordered script they used, codes can be added in adjacent rows to show the type and identity of each item the informants in that block responded to (see Figure 19).

The codes entered above the data for each group of informants can now be used to control sort operations along the rows. By sorting according to sentence number (or token set number), all of the rows are aligned such that all of the responses for any given sentence (or token set) appear in the same column of the table (see Figure 20). At this stage, the data are ready for preliminary statistical analysis. At this point, the data table should be preserved and further analysis done on a copy.

Figure 19 (Sample Data — "Data with Codes" sheet):

	A	B	C	D	E	F	G	R	S	T	U	V	W	X	Y	Z	AA	AB	AC	AD	AE	AF	AG	AH	AI	AJ	AK	AL	AM	AN	AO
2		INST	TYPE	D		NS	R1	R12	S1	S2	S3	S4	S5	S6	S7	S8	S9	S10	S11	S12	S13	S14	S15	S16	S17	S18	S19	S20	S21	S22	S23	S24
4				Codes →					p	p	c	d	p	p	a	b	p	a	p	d	b	p	c	c	p	p	d	b	p	a	p
5				→					16	43	7	6	56	33	4	12	14	9	23	3	2	44	5	54	1	24	15	10	11	55	8	34
6	A	A	0360	0		5	3		9	7	3	0	8	4	7	2	5	7	6	4	4	9	9	7	9	6	6	0	8	0	0	7
7	B	A	1350	0		7	0		9	9	7	0	9	1	9	0	9	9	9	1	0	9	9	9	8	2	9	0	9	0	7	9
8	B	A	6374	0		7	4		7	3	5	8	5	3	1	5	6	6	4	3	8	8	8	7	7	7	4	7	1	3	8	
10				Codes →					p	a	c	b	p	p	d	p	c	p	p	d	a	p	p	b	p	c	b	p	d	a	p	p
11				→					15	6	2	9	43	23	5	56	11	54	16	7	10	14	24	4	33	12	8	55	1	3	34	44
12	A	B	3264	0		0	4		7	4	3	3	5	5	5	3	2	2	5		6	2	2	6	6	0	7	7	7	7	7	7
13	A	B	9650	0		9	0		0	9	9	9	9	0	9	0	9	9	5	9	5	9	9	0	0	9	5	5	9	0	9	9
14	B	B	5474	0		5	1		0	9	7	7	2	4	3	2	6	3	1	4	2	9	7	2	9	7	4	1	0	4	9	6
15	B	B	5658	0		0	1		1	0	0	0	0	1	1	1	1	0	1	1	1	0	0	1	0	0	1	1	0	1	0	1
17				Codes →					p	p	c	b	p	a	d	p	c	a	p	b	p	c	a	p	p	c	a	p	b	d	p
18				→					24	33	8	3	15	7	2	44	11	4	16	56	5	55	10	14	54	43	9	1	23	6	12	34
19	A	C	7066	0		9	3		7	2	8	2	8	9	4	7	6	0	1	9	5	9	8	4	8	9	9	2	9	6	8	0
20	B	C	7374	0		4	3		8	2	4	3	9	8	5	3	4	4	2	9	6	9	6	8	5	8	0	9	4	7	2	

(sheet tabs: Data / Codes / Data with Codes)

Figure 19. Data with informants grouped such that all those who used a particular questionnaire appear together, and with coding information about the questionnaire added.

NOTE: Sentence types *a* through *d* are the experimental sentence types, and type *p* sentences are the fillers. The numerical codes (the second row of code data) are ID numbers for individual sentences. Thus the first item in the series S1–S24 for informants who used Questionnaire A was Filler Sentence 16, the second was Filler 43, and the third was the sentence representing condition *c* from Token Set 7.

Figure 20 (Sample Data — "Sorted Data -- sentences" sheet):

	A	B	C	D	E	F	G	R	S	T	U	V	W	X	Y	Z	AA	AB	AC	AD	AE	AF	AG	AH	AI	AJ	AK	AL	AM	AN	AO
2		INST	TYPE	D		NS	R1	R12	S1	S2	S3	S4	S5	S6	S7	S8	S9	S10	S11	S12	S13	S14	S15	S16	S17	S18	S19	S20	S21	S22	S23	S24
5									a	a	a	b	b	b	c	c	c	d	d	d	p	p	p	p	p	p	p	p	p	p	p	p
									1	2	3	4	5	6	7	8	9	10	11	12	11	12	13	21	22	31	32	41	42	51	52	53
6	A	A	6374	0		7	4		8	7	7	6	7	3	5	6	7	8	8	8	5	8	7	7	5	3	1	1	3	4	4	5
7	A	A	0360	0		5	3		9	7	8	7	6	7	3	6	6	7	7	8	5	9	9	9	4	4	2	0	0	4	0	0
8	B	A	1350	0		7	0		9	9	9	9	9	9	7	9	2	9	9	9	9	9	9	8	1	0	0	0	7	1	0	0
10									b	b	b	c	c	c	d	d	d	a	a	a	p	p	p	p	p	p	p	p	p	p	p	p
11									4	5	6	7	8	9	10	11	12	11	12	13	21	22	31	32	41	42	51	52	53			
12	B	B	3264	0		0	4		2	5	0	3	7		2	7	5	2	3	7		7	3	4	2	6	7	7	5	7	5	6
13	A	B	5474	0		5	1		9	3	7	2	1	4	6	0	2	7	7	9		6	7	9	3	9	4	2	4	1	0	4	2
14	A	B	9650	0		9	0		9	9	9	0	5	9	9	9	9	9	9	9		9	9	9	9	0	5	5	0	5	0	0	0
15	B	B	5658	0		0	1		0	1	0	1	1	1	1	0	0	0	0	0		1	0	0	0	1	1	1	1	1	1	1	1
17									c	c	c	d	d	d	a	a	a	b	b	b	p	p	p	p	p	p	p	p	p	p	p	p
18									1	2	3	4	5	6	7	8	9	10	11	12	21	22	32	42	51	52	11	12	13	31	41	53
19	B	C	7374	0		4	3		4	4	3	7	8	6	4	8	9	9	9	8		8	5	2	2	3	4	5	9	9	6	2	0
20	A	C	7066	0		9	3		6	6	7	8	9	5	8	9	9	8	8	8		7	4	2	1	2	0	9	9	9	4	0	2

(sheet tabs: Data with Codes / Sorted Data -- sentences)

Figure 20. Sorted data.

NOTE: Each block of data has been sorted along the rows so that the result for any given sentence appears in the same column of the table for each informant. Thus the first data item in each row representing a response to an experimental sentence is that informant's response on some sentence from Token Set 1. Which sentence from Token Set 1 was used differs from block to block down the table, as the codes above the token set numbers indicate.

10.3 Keying and Verifying Unscannable Responses

When informants respond via line drawing, magnitude estimation, or any other procedure that results in unscannable hand-written responses, some quality control issues arise as to how the data are translated into an electronic form. In the case of line drawing, the lines (i.e., the individual responses) must be individually measured. This process is sufficiently error-prone that it is usually wise to have two different individuals independently measure and record the length of each line (without either measurer seeing the other's results at this stage). It will generally be most convenient to record line lengths in millimeters.

Hand-written line length data and magnitude estimation responses from informants must next be translated to electronic form. The handiest way to do this with contemporary technology is usually to key the data into a spreadsheet or a database program. Occasionally, it may be more convenient to enter the data into a word processing program (or text editor) and later copy this file into a spreadsheet (although the formatting of the data in the word processing program should anticipate how the data will be translated into the spreadsheet).

In any event, it is very difficult to key in a large number of values without error. Standard procedure in many commercial operations confronting comparable tasks is to have all the data entered twice by (ideally) different coders. Errors are rare enough that it is extremely unlikely that both passes through the data set will produce the same errors, whether the keyboarding is done by two individuals or one.

The resulting data sets can then be compared in a spreadsheet to identify discrepancies. The discrepant cases can then be examined individually to determine what the correct data entry is. This process, although somewhat labor-intensive, seems to be both more economical and more reliable than keyboarding the data once and then checking it carefully for entry errors.

Note

1. Where resources and personnel are available, scanning services can construct simple software routines that will provide output formatted more like the file in Figure 17. However, the scanning process (together with errors informants make) will almost always introduce errors and anomalies that must be corrected by hand before the data are processed further.

11

Summarizing
the Data

Two kinds of data summaries are needed for most experiments on judgments. A summary "by informants" averages each informant's responses within each of the several sentence type categories and usually also summarizes in some way each informant's responses to the filler and/or benchmark materials. The table that results from this kind of summary will have a unique row for each informant. Along each row there will be, at minimum, one or more items of identifying information for that informant and a series of means, each of which is the average of all of that informant's responses in one of the experimental conditions. If an experimenter is to do an analysis "by materials," a further summary is also needed in which each token set is treated as a unit. Here, the experimenter represents each token set as though it were a single entity that was tested under several different conditions (each condition corresponding to one of the different sentences in the token set). The table that results from this summary has essentially the same structure as that for a by-informants analysis (identifying information followed by means), except that each row represents one token set rather than one informant.

The raw data that go into these two different kinds of summaries are exactly the same. The by-informants summary enters each individual response score into a mean that estimates the acceptability of a given sentence type *for a given informant*, but effaces information about which particular sentence the response came from. The by-materials summary enters each response into a mean that estimates the acceptability of a particular sentence (of a given type), but effaces information about the individual informants that gave those responses. Each type of summary is illustrated and discussed in more detail below.[1]

11.1 By-Informants Summaries

In the simplest cases, the results of a judgment experiment can be reduced to a table in which each informant is represented by an ID number and the averages of the informant's responses in the experimental conditions. For example, in Figure 21, each value that appears in the column labeled *a* within the Summary Table is the mean of the three responses that appear in the columns AB:AD[2] at the right edge of the figure. Each value in the other columns in the Summary Table is likewise the mean of a group of individual responses that appears somewhere in the spreadsheet to the right of the region shown (the columns labeled *a . . . d* represent four experimental conditions and the columns labeled *p1 . . . p5* represent five categories of filler sentence). In this example, the minimal results table would reduce to the ID column and the four columns headed *a . . . d*. Often, however, this most basic information will be augmented by demographic information about the informant (the columns labeled INST, TYPE, and NS) and summaries of the informant's responses on the filler or benchmark sentences (as in *p1 . . . p5*).[3]

11.1.1 Percentile Summaries

When informants use a category scale, it is sometimes inappropriate to represent each informant by the mean of the informant's responses on that scale. As noted earlier, different points on the category

	INST	TYPE	ID	NS	R1	R12	Summary Table									S1	S2	S3
							a	b	c	d	p1	p2	p3	p4	p5	a	a	a
																1	2	3
6	B	0	6374	0	7	4	7.33	5.33	5.33	8.00	6.50	6.00	2.00	2.00	4.33	8	7	7
7	A	0	0360	0	5	3	8.00	6.67	5.00	7.33	7.67	6.50	3.00	0.00	1.33	9	7	8
8	B	0	1350	0	7	0	9.00	9.00	6.00	9.00	9.00	4.50	0.00	3.50	0.33	9	9	9
9	A	0	2280	1	6	6	4.00	1.67	0.67	4.33	9.00	9.00	2.00	0.00	0.67	9	1	2
11																a	a	a
12																10	11	12
13	A	1	3264	0	0	4	4.00	2.33	5.00	4.67	4.67	4.00	6.50	6.00	6.00	2	3	7
14	A	1	5474	0	5	1	7.67	6.33	2.33	2.67	7.33	6.00	3.00	2.50	2.00	7	7	9
15	B	1	9650	0	9	0	9.00	9.00	4.67	9.00	9.00	4.50	5.00	2.50	0.00	9	9	9
16	A	1	5658	0	0	1	0.00	0.33	1.00	0.33	0.33	0.00	1.00	1.00	1.00	0	0	0
18																a	a	a
19																7	8	9
20	A	2	7374	0	4	3	7.00	8.67	3.67	7.00	7.67	6.50	4.00	2.00	2.33	4	8	9
21	B	2	7066	0	9	3	8.67	8.00	6.33	7.33	9.00	5.50	3.00	0.50	1.33	8	9	9
22	A	2	6964	1	8	5	6.67	8.67	9.00	9.00	7.33	4.50	2.50	0.50	2.33	7	4	9
23	A	2	0662	1	4	2	1.67	1.00	3.00	2.33	0.67	1.00	1.50	1.00	0.67	4	1	0

Sorted Data - informants \ **Mn Summarized Data** / % Summa

Figure 21. Summarized data.

NOTE: The new columns that make up the Summary Table (Columns S:AA; compare with Figure 20 in Chapter 10) include summaries of informant responses in various sentence type categories (see text for details).

scale can have different meanings for different informants. A way to ameliorate these difficulties is to represent the results in terms of the percentage of each informant's responses that fell at or above a given scale value for each sentence type. In other words, we might represent the first informant in Figure 21 as having used a scale value of seven or higher 100% of the time in Category *a*, or, alternatively, as having used a scale value of eight or higher for 33% of the *a* cases. If this approach is used, the resulting table takes the same form as in Figure 21 except that percentage values appear in the Summary Table.

Percentile summaries are generally appropriate only where a category scale has been used and may be less than ideal even in these cases. Experience demonstrates that for any given sentence, the percentage of responses that will fall at either extreme of a category scale is sensitive to the overall quality of the list within which the target sentence is presented. If the list contains many sentences of low acceptability, the proportion of responses at the high end of the scale will increase for individual target sentences. However, the relative acceptability of various sentences within a list of target sentences seems to remain approximately constant whether the overall quality of the list of fillers within which the target sentences are embedded is high or low (see Cowart, 1994). One handicap associated with using percentile summaries is that many linguists are tempted to ascribe more significance to percentile results than is warranted. Many will expect sentences they regard as acceptable to get a strong majority of the highest possible responses, regardless of the content of the filler list.

Ratio scale procedures are not compatible with either simple averages of raw scores or the percentile method described above.

11.1.2 Standardizing Informants

Another way to minimize differences in the way informants use a scale is to convert scores expressed in terms of the original scale to standard scores, often termed z-scores (see Appendix A), whose values are readily interpreted relative to the overall distribution of an informant's results. Positive values lie above the informant's mean and negative values below. Whether positive or negative, values near zero lie close to the informant's mean while those greater than one lie one or more standard deviations away from the informant's mean, that is, they are (assuming that the informant's scores are approximately normally distributed) more extreme than most of the informant's scores. One particular value of z-scores in work on judgments is that they can help to focus discussion on relative acceptability rather than "absolute" acceptability defined in terms of the response scale the informant used.

Standard scores can be used with data obtained via either category scale or ratio scale procedures.

11.2 By-Materials Summaries

A by-materials summary of the data set is constructed along the vertical axis of tables like those used above. The ordering of sentences (or token sets) along each row is the same for all rows (e.g., rows 12:29 in Figure 22). The Summary Table at the top of Figure 22 shows the percentage of responses for each variant of each sentence that fell at or above eight on the ten-point scale used here. That is, for sentence *a* of Token Set 1, 100% of the responses were at eight or above. For

							S1	S2	S3	S4	S5	S6	S7	S8	S9	S10	S11	S12	S13	S14	S15
NST	TYPE	D	NS	R1	R12																
% at or above 8 →						a	100%	38%	75%	63%	50%	50%	13%	25%	13%	63%	75%	75%	55%	77%	68%
						b	63%	50%	50%	38%	25%	13%	50%	50%	38%	63%	63%	63%			
						c	25%	25%	50%	63%	75%	38%	63%	63%	88%	75%	88%	88%			
						d	86%	29%	71%	86%	71%	57%	57%	57%	86%	29%	43%	57%			
						a	a	a	b	b	b	c	c	c	d	d	d	p	p	p
						1	2	3	4	5	6	7	8	9	10	11	12	11	12	13
B	0	6374	0	7	4	9	8	8	7	8	4	4	7	8	9	9	9	6	9	1
A	0	0360	0	5	3	10	8	9	8	7	8	4	7	7	8	8	9	6	10	10
B	0	1350	0	7	0	10	10	10	10	10	10	8	10	3	10	10	10	10	10	10
A	0	2280	1	6	6	10	2	3	2	2	4	1	2	2	2	10	4	10	10	10
						b	b	b	c	c	c	d	d	d	a	a	a	p	p	p
						1	2	3	4	5	6	7	8	9	10	11	12	11	12	13
A	1	3264	0	0	4	3	6	1	4	8	1	3	8	6	3	4	8	8	4	5
A	1	5474	0	5	1	10	4	8	3	2	5	7	1	3	8	8	10	7	8	10
B	1	9650	0	9	0	10	10	10	1	6	10	10	10	10	10	10	10	10	10	10
A	1	5658	0	0	1	1	2	1	2	2	2	2	1	1	1	1	1	2	1	1
						c	c	c	d	d	d	a	a	a	b	b	b	p	p	p
						1	2	3	4	5	6	7	8	9	10	11	12	11	12	13
A	2	7374	0	4	3	5	5	4	8	9	7	5	9	10	10	10	9	6	10	10
B	2	7066	0	9	3	7	7	8	9	10	6	10	10	9	9	9	10	10	10	10
A	2	6964	1	8	5	10	10	10	10	10	10	8	5	10	9	10	10	10	10	5
A	2	0662	1	4	2	2	4	6	3	5	2	5	2	1	2	2	2	1	1	3

Sample Data — Summary Table

Tabs: Std Summed Data \ **% Summed Materials Data** / GeoM Summed Materials Dat

Figure 22. By-materials data summarized in percentile terms.

NOTE: The values in the Summary Table show the percentage of values that fall at or above a criterion value (eight in this case) for each version of each sentence.

sentence *b* of Token Set 2, 50% of the responses were at eight or above, and so on. A similar summary for some filler sentences is shown in columns AE:AG. Here, however, the summaries cover the entire experiment because every informant judged every filler sentence.

A percentile summary of by-materials data will be appropriate only where a category scale response procedure was used. Ratio scale data must be summarized across informants via other methods that are discussed in the next section.

It is generally inconvenient to do statistical analysis on a table that takes the form of the Summary Table in Figure 22. Once this table is constructed, it will usually be helpful to convert it to the form shown in Figure 23, where all the data for each token set appear on one row.

11.2.1 Geometric Means

Because ratio scale procedures allow individual informants to vary widely in the range of values they choose, summarizing across

	A	B	C	D	E	F	G	H
				Sample Data				
1								
2				**Summary Table**				
3								
4					**Version**			
5		Token Set		a	b	c	d	
6		S1		100%	63%	25%	86%	
7		S2		38%	50%	25%	29%	
8		S3		75%	50%	50%	71%	
9		S4		63%	38%	63%	86%	
10		S5		50%	25%	75%	71%	
11		S6		50%	13%	38%	57%	
12		S7		13%	50%	63%	57%	
13		S8		25%	50%	63%	57%	
14		S9		13%	38%	88%	86%	
15		S10		63%	63%	75%	29%	
16		S11		75%	63%	88%	43%	
17		S12		75%	63%	88%	57%	
18								
19								

% Sum Tbl Data / GeoM

Figure 23. By-materials data summarized in percentile terms and reformatted for statistical analysis.

NOTE: The values in the table are the same as those shown in Figure 22.

informants for a given sentence or token set cannot be done via the methods described above. The standard method in this case is a geometric mean.[4]

11.3 Summaries for Filler and Benchmark Data

Summaries of filler and benchmark data are generally straight-forward. If the list of fillers used is structured in some way (e.g., the fillers represent five different degrees of acceptability), the filler sentences need to be segregated and summarized in ways similar to those used for experimental sentences. The Summary Table in Figure 22 includes items summarizing results on different fillers (*p11, p12* and so on). Benchmark materials generally do not need to be summarized, although they will play a role in statistical analyses. Their uses mainly have to do with estimating the quality of performance from individual informants.

Notes

1. The terminology for the two kinds of analyses mentioned here varies somewhat in the literature. Analyses by informants are often called "by-subjects" analyses. By-materials analyses are often called "by-sentences" analyses or "by-items" analyses.

2. Spreadsheet columns, rows, cells, and ranges of cells are referred to by way of the marginal labels seen in Figure 21 and elsewhere. Thus "AB:AD" is a reference to the range that includes all of columns AB, AC, and AD. The uppermost left cell in every sheet, for example, is referred to as "cell A1." A range of cells is referenced by way of the upper left and lower right corners of the range. Thus "S6:V9" is a reference to the summaries of experimental data for the first four informants in Figure 21.

3. Each of the illustrations in this chapter will show only that portion of the relevant spreadsheet necessary to reveal the structure of that particular summary under discussion at that point. The complete spreadsheets are collected in an Excel workbook that is available at the Web site for this book, which can be found at HTTP://WWW.USM.MAINE.EDU/~LIN

4. See Section C.4 of Appendix C for instructions on calculating geometric means.

12

Statistical
Issues

If an experiment tests four different sentence types, it is not uncommon for there to be no two types with exactly the same average acceptability value. Some of these differences, however, may be small ones that do not reflect consistent differences between the two sentence types. Upon repeated testing, we might find no difference at all, or a small difference in the opposite direction. To interpret a numerical difference between the means for two sentence types, an investigator must decide whether or not to draw the inference that there is a consistent difference in acceptability between the two types for the tested individual or group. Although no procedure can guarantee the truth of the conclusions the investigator settles on, statistical tests do allow the investigator to impose controls on the likelihood of error. Statistical procedures cannot prevent investigators from drawing inferences that lead to errors, nor can they determine whether or not any particular inference leads to error, but, when carefully applied, they can give the investigator reasonable assurance that no more than a certain predetermined percentage of a set of statistically tested inferences do in fact lead to error. *Statistics,* as it is used here, is mostly about the rational control of error.[1]

This chapter has two purposes relative to the statistical issues that arise in studies of acceptability. For those investigators who are prepared to do appropriate statistical tests themselves, it will provide some guidance on the handling of certain statistical issues that arise in the context of research on judgments. For those who lack statistical training or experience, the chapter will offer some general guidance on where to find appropriate assistance or training.

12.1 Alternative Tests for Category Scale Data

In Chapter 6, we noted that category scale procedures do not always produce interval level data. In particular, there may be experimental circumstances where, for example, the difference in acceptability marked by scale scores of one and two on a five-point scale will be larger (or smaller) than the acceptability difference indicated by scores of four and five. Where this condition arises, the experiment has produced, strictly speaking, ordinal level data, not the interval level data that are assumed by most varieties of analysis of variance and related statistical tests. If analysis of variance and similar procedures are used with such data, the reliability of the tests themselves is uncertain.

Where a particular contrast is numerically large compared with variability around the relevant means, any statistical problems deriving from a failure to achieve interval level measurement are not likely to be consequential. There also may be circumstances where for practical reasons an investigator will choose to use a category scale procedure even when some small differences are expected.

In circumstances such as these, it is still reasonable and appropriate to apply standard ANOVA tests to the resulting data. However, a second kind of analysis ought to be used as well to ensure that any possible violation of ANOVA assumptions does not affect the outcome of the test.

This further test is based on a different summary of the data. Instead of constructing means, the initial summary calculates the percentage of responses that fell at or above some criterion in each informant's responses for each sentence type category. Thus, if the criterion were set at four and an informant judged six No "that"/Subject Extraction sentences on a scale of one to five, and rated two of those sentences at four or higher, then that informant's responses in that category would be summarized as 40%. This same kind of summary is then constructed for all other by-informants and by-materials analyses, and the same statistical tests as would be used otherwise are applied from this point on. This sort of data is guaranteed to meet the criteria for the interval level of measurement and thus does not threaten the integrity of ANOVA results. Any significant main effects or differences that emerge from summaries both by means and by percentages (of the sort suggested here) can be relied upon (with the usual caveats about meeting the assumptions of the tests). Any results that are significant in the means-based analysis, but not in the percentages-based analysis, are suspect. In such a case, it would be appropriate to do a further experiment, perhaps on a smaller scale, using a ratio scale technique.

The main disadvantage of percentage summaries is that they waste information. These summaries have no way to capture information about how an informant's responses are distributed above and below the chosen criterion. Thus these summaries will generally be less sensitive. For any given sample size, there will be small differences that can be detected with tests based on a means summary, but not with a percentages summary. Nevertheless, this approach is useful as a backup to standard statistical procedures where an investigator chooses to use a category scale technique.

12.2 Testing Generalizations Across Informants and Token Sets

As illustrated in Chapter 11, usually the results of any experiment designed along the lines described in this book can be summarized in two ways. One way summarizes the results by informants, providing a mean judged acceptability value for each token type for each informant. Another way summarizes the results by token set, providing mean judged acceptability values for each sentence in each token set (Clark, 1973).[2] For the most part, the same statistical tests are then applied to the token set data as are applied to the informant data. Clark's paper provides relatively simple methods for integrating tests on informant data and token set data (in his terms, by-subjects data and by-items data) such that an investigator can report a single *t*-test or ANOVA result covering both analyses. This practice, however, has met with far less than universal acceptance. When investigators do both kinds of tests, they quite commonly report the informants and sentences tests separately. Tests done on summaries by informant are usually presented with a subscript "1" appended (e.g., F_1) and summaries by token set have a subscript "2."

The rationale for doing both kinds of test is that, just as the informants actually tested in an experiment are (usually) seen as representatives of the entire population from which they are selected, the token sets are likewise seen as representatives of all the relevantly similar token sets one might construct in the same language (or perhaps any language). Just as statistical tests on data for informants test the reliability of patterns seen in those results, so tests on data for token sets test the reliability of patterns seen in the summaries of the token set data. Most often the two kinds of tests produce virtually identical results, but especially where weak or marginal effects are involved, it is worthwhile to ask whether an effect is reliable across both informants and token sets. Many experiments incorporate one or more factors that cannot be tested in both analyses.

The analogy between informants and token sets is hardly perfect, and the analogy between the notion of a population of people and a population of token sets is shakier still. Thus it is not obvious that statistical tests that are meant to test generalizations across populations are being used equally appropriately in these two cases. Chomsky's (1986) suggestion that languages exist only as patterns of behavior projected from the internal states of speakers can only raise further doubts; in Chomsky's view, it appears that there is no population from which to sample. Nevertheless, Clark's recommendation that both kinds of test be done is often sound. There is no doubt that experimental results on language are sometimes misinterpreted as applying generally to all similar linguistic materials when all that has been shown is that the result is reliable only when exactly the same materials are used.

12.3 Variation Accounted For

Statistical tests of significance can be given greater weight than they deserve. There are limitations associated with these measures that need to be kept in view. Fortunately, there are also some additional measures that can be derived from *t*-tests and analysis of variance that help to ameliorate some of these limitations.

There is a sense in which significant results from *t*-tests or ANOVAs can be highly reliable, but uninformative. It is entirely possible, and often happens, that an ANOVA will detect a reliable effect due to some manipulation in an experiment where that manipulation has only a very tiny impact on the performance of subjects. Manipulations that control only a very small share of the variance in an experiment, even where they are reliable, are relatively uninformative. Most of the variance is being affected by something, but it isn't the factor we are manipulating.

It is also worth bearing in mind that the standard statistical sense of "significant" has no necessary connection to questions about theoretical importance. Differences may be simultaneously significant (from a statistical point of view) and boring (from a theoretical point of view). Whether a statistically significant difference matters in some larger sense can only be determined by examining its relevance to alternative theories that bear on the situation in which the difference arises.

Especially with a particularly stable phenomenon such as sentence judgments seem to be, there is a somewhat arbitrary lower limit on the size of the effects that can be found significant.[3] By increasing sample size, progressively more and more delicate reliable differences can be detected. For example, in our work on "that"-trace, it is possible to detect a tiny but reliable difference in acceptability between subject extraction and object extraction when no "that" is present, provided that (by combining results from two large experiments) we attain a sample size of more than 1,100. Although it seems obvious that this finding is of no theoretical interest, it raises the question of how experimenters are to estimate which statistically significant effects are also significant in a more general theoretical sense.

A statistic that responds to this need is η^2 (see Appendix A for information on calculating η^2). This value indicates the share of all the variation in a data set that is accounted for by a particular factor in an experimental design. Thus, in an analysis of a "that"-trace experiment, we can calculate the percentage of all the variation in the result that is due to the "that" effect, to the interaction, and so on. Data from analyses of two of the "that"-trace experiments mentioned

Table 14 F and η^2 statistics for two "that"-trace experiments.

	Experiment 1 (N = 32)		Experiment 2 (N = 332)	
	F	η^2	F	η^2
"That" Effect	63.5	43%	690	34%
Extraction Site	29.6	8%	282	11%
Interaction	27.1	9%	361	13%

earlier appear in Table 14. Here the second experiment, with roughly ten times more informants, is obviously much more sensitive. The F values are about ten times larger than those of the first experiment. This suggests that if there were any smaller, weaker effects in the same design, the second experiment would be more likely to detect significant differences for those effects. Note, however, that the values of η^2 are roughly similar for the three factors despite the 1:10 difference in F values.

In fact, there were some weak effects associated with a "groups" factor in this experiment. This was a between-informants factor in which individuals were categorized according to which of four versions of the questionnaire they responded to. Although there were no significant effects associated with this factor in the first experiment, there were two reliable interactions with this factor in the second experiment. However, η^2 showed that each of these interactions accounted for only about one half of 1% of the variation in the experiment. Thus, although both were quite reliable, neither is of any theoretical interest because they account for such a very small share of the overall variation, compared with the effects listed in Table 14.

Another application of η^2 to the same two experiments appears in Figure 24. Here η^2 has been applied to comparisons between four particular pairs of means within the larger design. Each of these individual tests is logically equivalent to a t-test covering only two means. In these cases, the values indicate how much of the variation in the informant means underlying the overall means is accounted for by the contrast between the conditions, as opposed to error variance within the conditions. Note, as before, that despite the fact that Experiment 2 employed far more informants, the η^2 values are generally similar, although the effect of having or not having "that" in the object extraction cases was larger in the first experiment.

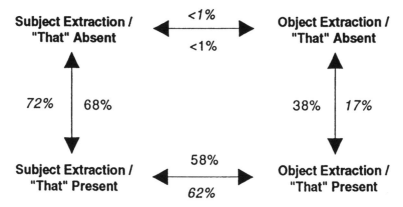

Figure 24. Comparison of variation accounted for in four pairwise comparisons in two "that"-trace experiments.

NOTE: The four innermost percentage figures show η^2 values for four pairwise comparisons from Experiment 1 in Table 14. The italicized outermost values are the corresponding values for Experiment 2.

Perhaps the best description of the role of η^2 is that it provides an index of the informativeness of significant effects in ANOVAs, *t*-tests, and related procedures. If the manipulations applied in an experiment produce reliable effects, but those reliable effects don't control much of the variance in an experiment, we do not learn much from knowing that the effect is reliable. If, on the other hand, an effect is reliable and accounts for a large share of the variance in the experiment (even if the difference in means associated with it is small), then we know a good deal more. We know that there is a manipulation that has an impact; we have found a factor that changes something and we have gained greater insight into the phenomenon at hand.

These suggestions also show how η^2 can resolve the problem mentioned earlier where, by combining two large "that"-trace experiments, we were able to detect a reliable difference between subject extraction and object extraction with "that" absent. Although reliable when tested by way of a huge experiment, the pairwise comparison between these means accounts for only about one third of 1% of the variation, even within just the pairwise test. Thus η^2 provides clear grounds for dismissing this "significant" effect; it is of no theoretical interest, however reliable it may be, because we learn nothing from it.

12.4 Getting Training or Assistance in Statistics

One way investigators who lack training or experience in statistical methods may apply the methods described in this book is to
seek assistance from a statistician or statistical consulting service.
Such services are available on many college and university campuses, often without charge. There is an enormous variety of different statistical techniques available and not all statisticians are equally
familiar with all of these methods. Someone familiar with factorial
repeated measures analysis of variance designs is most likely to be
helpful. Statisticians who work frequently with experimental psychologists are likely to be familiar with all or most of the tests and
procedures mentioned in this book.

Investigators who want to undertake a study of statistics for
themselves should plan on working through a body of material
roughly equivalent to two courses. Analysis of variance is considered
a somewhat advanced technique, and introductory courses (and
texts) rarely give it more than a relatively brief introductory treatment. There are countless introductory statistics texts available, some
of which have been designed for self-study. To lay a foundation for
the methods used here, a statistical novice should look for a text that
covers basic descriptive statistics and graphing, basic inferential
statistics (z-tests, t-tests), elementary analysis of variance, and correlation. A variety of advanced texts in analysis of variance are also
available.

A number of statistical software packages are available for personal computers. Access to one of these is essential. The volume of data
in even modest-sized acceptability experiments quickly overcomes the
practical limits of calculators. Not all statistical packages that incorporate some analysis of variance routines support the factorial within-sub-
jects (or repeated measures) designs applied here.

Notes

1. This sentence includes a near quote of a scholar to whom I owe a considerable debt but whose identity I have lost track of.
2. Clark (1973) pointed out that many prior experimental studies using linguistic materials had failed to establish the generality of their linguistic claims. It was at
that time common for investigators to (implicitly) assume that all relevantly similar
linguistic materials would produce the same results as those actually used in a given

study. Yet an experiment that compared some aspect of performance with nouns and verbs necessarily would employ only some rather small sampling of actual nouns and verbs in the relevant language. Clark pointed out that results obtained in this way could not support generalizations stated in terms of linguistic categories unless appropriate statistical tests were run on the linguistic materials themselves, as well as on the human subjects of the experiment. In the absence of such tests, scrupulous investigators would confine their claims of generality to people (e.g., "Subjects identify < *list of specific words* > more rapidly than < *list of specific words* >") and avoid statistically untested linguistic generalizations (e.g., "Subjects identify *high frequency nouns* more rapidly than *low frequency nouns*"). This of course would be unsatisfactory for most studies bearing on linguistic materials, so Clark went on to suggest specific statistical methods that could be used in cases where an investigator wishes to generalize simultaneously to a human population and to a "population" of linguistic materials. Clark's point has been widely accepted, although the particular statistical solutions he advocated have enjoyed less success.

3. In statistics, effect size is not to be confused with the size of the numerical difference between two means. For a *t*-test, for example, effect size is a ratio between the difference between the means and the variability around those means. Large numerical differences can be associated with high variability and thus small effect size and numerically small differences between two means can be associated with little variation and correspondingly large effect size.

Appendix A:
A Reader's Guide
to Statistics

The purpose of this appendix is to provide some brief background material on some statistical concepts and tools that are used in this book. This will not replace the full treatment of these notions in an appropriate text, but it should give readers without prior background a better basis on which to interpret the statistical findings reported here.

It is useful to distinguish between descriptive and inferential statistical procedures. Where descriptive statistics are useful for stating or describing some property of a sample (e.g., the location or dispersion of a set of measurements on a group of individuals), inferential statistics aid investigators in determining which inferences about the larger population from which the sample was drawn are and are not warranted by a given pattern of results. This appendix will first review some basic descriptive tools that are used in the book and then turn to brief discussions of some standard inferential statistics.

A.1 Descriptive Tools

A.1.1 Measures of Central Tendency

The most common measure of central tendency for a set of judgments is the *mean* or arithmetic average. The experiments discussed in this book invariably involve collecting responses in two or more different conditions and comparing the means of the responses in those conditions. One generally desirable property of the mean is that it is sensitive to all the measurements in the sample. This property is sometimes undesirable if there are one or more outliers (extreme measurements that lie far from most other measurements), or if the set of measurements is skewed (scores are heavily clustered toward the high or low end of the used range). In these cases, a useful alternative index of central tendency is the *median*, which is the score value that cuts the distribution of scores in half. If a distribution consisted of values 3, 4, 6, 8, 9, and 26, the median would be 7 because half the scores fall on either side of this value. The *geometric mean* is useful in circumstances where a set of measurements comes from individuals who vary considerably in average response. Thus, in averaging responses from three individuals who have mean response levels of 3, 4.5, and 34, the geometric mean, like the median, will reduce sensitivity to the distorting effects of extreme values.

A.1.2 Standard Deviation

One of the principal concerns in any statistical characterization of a set of scores is the degree of dispersion or variation that occurs within those scores. The most common statistic for describing this property is the standard deviation. In a normally distributed set of scores (i.e., one that has the shape of the familiar "bell curve"), a little more than two thirds of all the scores will lie within one standard deviation unit above or below the mean. Thus a sample for which the standard deviation value is large is one where the scores are more widely distributed than one where the standard deviation value is small.

A.1.3 Standard Scores/z-Scores

Individual informants sometimes use a single response measure in different ways. The average of all of an informant's values will differ from informant to informant and the responses of some informants will be more widely distributed across the available range than will those of another. Standard scores (also called "z-scores") are a common tool for correcting for these sorts of differences. To convert an original raw score value to a standard score, the score is expressed as a distance above or below the mean, measured in standard deviation units. Thus a standard score value of 1.0 represents a score that is one standard deviation unit above the relevant mean. A standard score of –2.5 represents a score that is two and one half standard deviation units below the mean. When a set of scores is standardized (i.e., converted to z-scores), the mean of the set of standardized scores will always be 0 and the standard deviation of the set of standardized scores will be 1. Thus, when the data from each individual informant in a sample are standardized, all informants now have the same mean and standard deviation. Note, however, that this procedure loses no information about the distribution of the informant's scores; the pattern of the informant's scores is completely preserved by this transformation.

A.1.4 Standard Error of the Mean

One of the essential insights exploited in inferential statistics is the observation that the variability of a set of scores in a single sample can be used to estimate the scattering of sample means that would occur if many similar samples were drawn from the same population. This insight underlies a measure called the standard error of the mean. This value plays a somewhat similar role for a (usually hypothetical) collection of sample means that the standard deviation plays for a set of scores. If repeated samples of the same size were drawn from a population having the same mean and standard deviation as does the actual sample, then a little more than two thirds of all the new samples would have means within a range spanning one standard error unit above and below the given mean. Thus a mean associated with a small standard error value is one that lies close to the true mean of the measured population while one associated with a large standard error value is one that may lie further from the population's true mean.

A.2 Inferential Statistics

In the experiments described in this book, the goal is to estimate some property or parameter of a population on the strength of the sample from that population that was actually tested in each experiment. Thus our goal is typically to determine whether responses to Sentence Type A indicate greater or lesser acceptability *in the relevant population* than do responses to Sentence Type B. Given that experiments will almost always yield at least some small numerical difference between any two conditions, the basic problem of inferential statistics is to provide investigators with some systematic guidance as to when it is or is not appropriate to draw the inference that there is also a consistent difference between the measured conditions in the target population.

There are two kinds of error an investigator may make in decisions of this kind. Type I errors are those where the investigator credits too small a difference. That is, the investigator detects a difference between two conditions in an experiment and draws the inference that there is a reliable difference between the two conditions in the target population when in fact there is no such difference. Type II errors are those where the investigator fails to credit a difference detected in an experiment and falsely concludes that there is no difference in the target population. Unfortunately, the likelihood of each of these two kinds of error is often linked. Insurance against making one kind can sometimes only be purchased by increasing the chance of making the other. Increasing sample size can reduce the probability of both kinds of error.

The test statistics used in this book address this dilemma by trying to estimate the likelihood of the actually obtained data, given some baseline hypothesis about conditions in the tested population. Thus, if an investigator is interested in the relative acceptability of Sentence Type A and Sentence Type B, *and if there is actually no difference between these two in the target population,* how likely is it that the experiment could have produced the differences in average measured acceptability that actually appeared in the experiment? This estimate is derived from the variability of the obtained sample. That is, the variability within and between individuals within the actual sample provides an estimate of the variability within the population as a whole. From this it is possible to calculate how likely it is that differences in means of the obtained size could have arisen if in fact there were no differences in these means in the population. When, by procedures of this kind, we are able to show that the obtained differences are very unlikely were there no real differences in the population, we generally say that the obtained difference is (statistically) significant, although perhaps it is more helpful to say that we have evidence that the difference between the tested means is reliable.

A.2.1 *t-Tests*

One of the more elementary applications of this logic arises in a family of inferential statistics call *t-tests*, which compare only two means and are generally reported in a form like the following: "Sentence Type A is more acceptable than Sentence Type B, $t(26) = 2.82, p < .01$." Here, "26" indicates the degrees of freedom of the test (related to sample size). The notation "$p < .01$" provides the most critical piece of information. This value indicates how likely it is that the actual obtained result (the observed difference between the two means) would have arisen if in fact there were no difference between these conditions in the target population. Obviously, small p values underwrite confidence that the obtained difference is reliable and large values (commonly considered to be those above .05, although important complexities are being set aside here) suggest that the obtained differences between the means could have relatively easily arisen by chance.

A.2.2 Analysis of Variance

Analysis of variance is a more varied and versatile family of procedures, although the underlying logic is the same as that of the *t*-test. The difference is that where *t*-tests apply only to pairs of means, analysis of variance (or, commonly, ANOVA) procedures allow an investigator to make many comparisons within a single data set simultaneously. Thus all of the "that"-trace experiments discussed in this book can be seen as two simultaneous and overlapped pairwise experiments. One experiment compares sentences with and without "that" and one compares those exhibiting subject extraction with those exhibiting object extraction. By integrating these two into a single experiment, it becomes possible to overcome a difficulty that would arise if two or more different *t*-tests were done on the same data set. *If for any one* t-test we set a threshold value (α in the statistics literature) of .05, allowing ourselves to credit an obtained difference that falls at or below this threshold and rejecting any result that falls above it, we have ensured that the likelihood of error in drawing an inference from our result is .05 or less. However, if we conduct 20 experiments, each comparing some pair of means, and in each case we find that the obtained p value is at or just below .05, then the odds are that somewhere in the set of 20 comparisons there is an error. Thus the overall chance of making an erroneous inference is not 1:20, as it is for each individual experiment, but approximately 1:1. That is, we are highly likely to have drawn at least one erroneous inference in the set of 20. ANOVA techniques make it possible for an investigator to apply overall control to a set of comparisons so that the threshold value the investigator selects at the outset is the one that actually obtains in the analysis of results.

Another very valuable feature of ANOVA techniques is that they can compare not just two but many related means at once. Thus one experiment described in Chapter 1 includes a definiteness factor that has four different "levels" (roughly equivalent to a t-test that simultaneously compares four means, asking whether any one or more of them is reliably different than any other). A further very valuable class of ANOVA designs allow investigators to examine interactions among two or more effects. That is, as happens in the "that"-trace experiments discussed in this book, one effect (subject extraction versus object extraction) has a very different impact on acceptability depending upon which "level" of the other factor ("that" present versus absent) is involved. When no "that" is present, the subject versus object extraction effect is negligible, and when "that" is present, it is large. ANOVA procedures make it possible to assess the reliability of this sort of interaction effect alongside simpler comparisons.

ANOVA results are reported in a format similar to that for t-tests. In general, an identification of the effect or interaction is followed by a summary statement of the statistical result, as in the following: "The interaction between the Extraction Site and 'That' factors was reliable, $F(1, 22) = 8.03, p < .01$." The notation "(1, 22)" specifies the degrees of freedom for the test, there being two values because the F statistic is a ratio. The degrees of freedom of the test is again related to sample size, but that relation is much less straightforward in analyses of variance. As with the t-test, the critical piece of information is the p value, which here indicates that the observed pattern of data is very unlikely on the assumption that there is no difference in the sampled population. F-tests that fail to indicate reliable results are generally reported with the notation "NS" in place of the p value, or sometimes with no probability statement at all if the F-value is small (e.g., $F < 1$).

A.2.3 Assumptions Underlying Inferential Statistics

Inferential statistics are invariably defined in terms of a mathematical model of the situation in which the obtained data arise. These models make assumptions about conditions in the experiment that do not necessarily accurately reflect the true state of affairs. The most sophisticated consumers of statistical results often will want to ask whether the data set under consideration in a particular case in fact met all of the assumptions of the tests that were applied to it. In the context of this book, perhaps the most important assumption of this kind is the assumption, common to most ANOVA techniques, that the data achieve what is called the interval level of measurement. This notion is examined in more detail in Chapter 6. The most common varieties of ANOVA test also assume (among other things) that the data are more or less normally distributed and that variances are approximately equal across various conditions.

A.2.4 Correlation Coefficients

The most common correlation coefficient, Pearson's r, provides an index of how closely two continuous variables track each other. Pearson's r ranges from -1 to 1, with larger positive values indicating a strong direct relation between the two variables and negative values indicating that the values are inversely related (an increase in one predicts a decrease in the other). If, for example, we collected many samples of vowel sounds, then directly measured fundamental frequency for each of those sounds and by other means measured the average spacing between harmonics in those sounds, we expect these two values to be very closely related; in general, we should be able to predict one measurement from the other. If our expectation is upheld, Pearson's r will show a large positive value. Large numerical values (regardless of sign) indicate a strong relation between the tested variables.

The reliability of the relation between two variables can be tested. In effect, this test asks how likely it is that the obtained data would have arisen if in fact there were no relation between the two variables in the sampled population. Where this test is applied to an r value, usually degrees of freedom, "df" will be reported (reflecting the number of pairs of values tested) along with a p value, as in the

Table 15 Calculation of η^2.

Source	SS	DF	MS	F	η^2
"That"	2.0187	1	2.0187	48.7	.26
Error	1.0365	25	0.0415		
Extraction Site	1.5899	1	1.5899	37.7	.21
Error	1.0548	25	0.0422		
Interaction	1.1691	1	1.1691	35.5	.15
Error	0.8235	25	0.0329		
Total sum of squares	7.6925				

following: "The fundamental frequency and harmonic spacing measurements were closely related, $r = .98$, df = 42, $p < .001$."

A.2.5 Percentage of Variability Accounted For

Very often, correlation statistics are reported in terms of r^2 rather than r. The advantage of this statistic is that it has a much more straightforward and intuitive interpretation than does r itself. The r^2 statistic can be interpreted as a direct measure of the proportion of the variability in one measure that is accounted for by variability on the other. In other words, once the variability of one of two correlated measures is known, a certain proportion of the variability on the other becomes predictable and r^2 gives a measure of that proportion.

A related statistic can also be computed for factors and interactions in ANOVAs. Termed η^2, this value measures the proportion of the total variability in an experiment that is attributable to the indicated factor or interaction. Thus, if an experiment included a factor of "Complexity" (having, say, two levels), and that factor is associated with an η^2 value of .42, we conclude that 42% of the total variability in the experiment is due to the manipulation of degrees of complexity.

The calculation of η^2 is quite straightforward. As illustrated in Table 15, the sum of squares (SS) for each factor or interaction in the ANOVA result table is divided by the total sum of squares for the data set as a whole.

Appendix B: Statistical Supplement to Chapter 1

This appendix reports on the statistical tests that were applied to the various experiments discussed in Chapter 1. The appendix is organized under subheads relating to the sections of Chapter 1. Readers unfamiliar with the statistical terms used in this appendix will find some notes on the purpose and interpretation of these measures in Appendix A.

Clark (1973) argues that many experiments on linguistic materials should be tested for their generality across both subjects or informants and linguistic materials (see Chapter 12 for further discussion). Clark's recommendation is generally followed here. Statistical tests done on summaries by informant have a subscript "1" appended (e.g., F_1) and summaries by token set have a subscript "2" appended. Significance levels are indicated by asterisks: "*" for $p < .05$, "**" for $p < .01$, and "***" for $p < .001$. Where appropriate, the results reported below will be expressed in terms of standard score (z-score) units.

B.1 Subjacency

The overall main effect in ANOVA testing differences among the four conditions was significant, $F_1(3, 261) = 194$***, $F_2(3, 69) = 90.9$***.

The main effect of Definiteness accounted for 69% of overall variance in the experiment.

Each of the pairwise differences in Figure 2 from left to right is significant; $F_1(1, 87) = 132^{***}$, $F_2(1, 23) = 50.1^{***}$ for the control/indefinite contrast, $F_1(1, 87) = 62.7^{***}$, $F_2(1, 23) = 31.7^{***}$ for the indefinite/definite contrast, and $F_1(1, 87) = 11.5^{**}$, $F_2(1, 23) = 8.15^{**}$ for the definite/specified subject contrast.

In the second subjacency experiment (described in Figure 3), the contrast between the Indefinite/"of" cases and the Control was significant, $F_1(1, 40) = 46.6^{***}$, but the contrast with the Indefinite/"to" cases was also robust, $F_1(1, 40) = 16.9^{***}$. There was no significant difference between the two cases ending in "to." The overall pattern of results was also significant, $F_1(3, 120) = 17.1^{***}$.[1]

There are some reasons to doubt that category scale procedures such as those used for the experiments reported in this section reliably produce interval level data (see Chapter 6). There is at least one way, however, to use category scale results that ensures that the interval level of measurement is achieved. Instead of calculating the mean within each category of an informant's responses, the investigator summarizes the data by calculating the percentage of responses in each category that are at or above some criterial level. Thus we can determine what percentage of trials within a given category produced the highest possible response and use this value in further analysis.[2] This is, however, a very wasteful procedure. It loses all the information encoded in the different specific score values that informants used.

Applying this approach to the experimental results described above yields an outcome similar to the earlier analysis. The main effect is significant, $F_1(3, 261) = 128^{***}$, $F_2(3, 69) = 56.0^{***}$. Likewise, each of the pairwise differences from left to right is significant; $F_1(1, 87) = 135^{***}$, $F_2(1, 23) = 34.7^{***}$ for the control/indefinite contrast, $F_1(1, 87) = 5.97^{*}$, $F_2(1, 23) = 9.31^{**}$ for the indefinite/definite contrast, and $F_1(1, 87) = 16.2^{***}$, $F_2(1, 23) = 4.67^{*}$ for the definite/specified subject contrast.

B.2 "That"-Trace

Eight different pseudorandom orderings of the materials were used in this experiment.

For the results summarized in Figure 4, there is no difference in acceptability between Subject and Object Extraction in the absence of "that," but there is such a difference (favoring Object Extraction) in the presence of "that." This difference was reflected in the interaction between Extraction Site and the Presence/Absence of "that," $F_1(1, 31) = 30.3^{***}$, $F_2(1, 23) = 22.4^{***}$, and in overall main effects of Extraction Site, $F_1(1, 31) = 31.7^{***}$, $F_2(1, 23) = 10.8^{**}$, and Presence/Absence of "that," $F_1(1, 31) = 96.0^{***}$, $F_2(1, 23) = 72.6^{***}$. Although the pairwise comparison of the two cases with "that" is significant, $F_1(1, 31) = 53.4^{***}$, $F_2(1, 23) = 26.1^{***}$, there is obviously no difference between the two cases without "that," $F_{1, 2} < 1$. Note also that there is a "that"-effect that co-occurs with the "that"-trace effect. Object Extraction in cases with "that" is substantially less acceptable than is extraction without "that," $F_1(1, 31) = 20.0^{***}$, $F_2(1, 23) = 8.28^{**}$.

B.3 Coordination and Binding Theory

The findings summarized in Figure 5 confirm the influence of the Binding Theory in all three pairs of cases. The main effect of Antecedent Location (Local versus Remote) is significant overall, $F_1(1, 41) = 125^{***}$, $F_2(1, 23) = 131^{***}$, and in each of the three contexts, No Coordination, $F_1(1, 42) = 207^{***}$, $F_2(1, 23) = 151^{***}$, Simple Coordination, $F_1(1, 42) = 54.8^{***}$, $F_2(1, 23) = 72.6^{***}$, and "Both" Coordination, $F_1(1, 42) = 19.9^{***}$, $F_2(1, 23) = 9.69^{**}$.

There was a reliable interaction between the Antecedent Location and Context factors, $F_1(2, 84) = 28.9^{***}$, $F_2(2, 46) = 22.5^{***}$, and a main effect for Context, $F_1(2, 84) = 23.6^{***}$, $F_2(2, 46) = 11.6^{***}$. Looking only at the Remote Antecedent cases, there was a significant increase in acceptability from the No Coordination condition to the Simple Coordination condition, $F_1(1, 42) = 23.7^{***}$, $F_2(1, 23) = 13.8^{**}$, and from the Simple Coordination condition to the "Both" Coordination condition, $F_1(1, 42) = 19.6^{***}$, $F_2(1, 23) = 14.6^{***}$.

B.4 Stability of Responses to Individual Sentences

Correlation tests within the two subsets of filler sentences confirmed the impression of Figure 7; there was a strong correlation between First and Second Session ratings for both the High Acceptability items, $F(1, 62) = 140^{***}$, $r^2 = .70$, and for the Low Acceptability items, $F(1, 30) = 76.3^{***}$, $r^2 = .72$.

Notes

1. The original data set for this experiment is no longer available; no analysis by materials was done.

2. Other criteria can also be used, such as the percentage of responses that fall in the two highest categories or the percentage in the lowest category.

Appendix C: Excel as a Syntactician's Workbench

This appendix provides information on how Microsoft Excel (version 5), a spreadsheet program, can be used to construct and analyze experiments on sentence acceptability. Although Excel's primary applications are quantitative, it includes a rich set of text functions that support the manipulations needed in constructing sentence materials. A spreadsheet is, of course, a natural tool to use for the extensive data manipulation process that intervenes between data collection and statistical analysis. I have adopted Excel as a frame of reference for the discussion here because it is available in nearly identical form for both Macintosh and Windows systems, is widely used on both those platforms, and is supported by extensive third party documentation. Because Excel (and its companion, Microsoft Word) can work with a wide variety of fonts and is compatible with multilingual technologies on both the Macintosh and the Windows platforms, the approaches described here are also applicable to work on languages using a variety of orthographies. Note, however, that the solutions to the practical problems presented here are far from unique. Many other approaches are possible within the framework assumed here and a variety of other software tools provide similar functions or alternative functions that could achieve similar results. The particular processes and approaches described here are meant to strike a balance between efficiency and intelligibility. Experienced investigators may well want to alter or adapt these procedures to better suit their individual needs.

Excel also incorporates (as do all widely used spreadsheet programs) a macro language (Visual Basic) that allows users to automate repetitive tasks. In some cases, this facility can be applied via a "show me" method where the user simply executes the process in question while Excel "watches" (i.e., records the process as a series of program steps that can later be applied to other cases). This appendix will be concerned only with "manual" methods because these are more readily adapted to a variety of goals and research designs, but where an investigator uses certain methods frequently on files of fairly constant structure, there are ways to automate these methods that can provide significant time savings.

The appendix does *not* include basic training on Excel. A wide variety of tutorial and reference materials are currently available, including works that are aimed at users at every level of expertise (or lack thereof). Most large bookstores (on campus and off) will carry a substantial assortment of these materials. This appendix will assume knowledge of terms and processes that are covered in standard tutorial materials on Excel.

The processes I will describe below have many steps. It will be wise to save files often and to preserve intermediate steps in the process so that later errors can be corrected without beginning from scratch again.

The examples and illustrations provided below will often assume a 2×2 experimental design such as is applied in the "that"-trace experiments discussed in the book. The process of adapting these procedures to other designs is generally straightforward, although novices may want to stay relatively close to the examples in their early efforts.

C.1 Accessing Software Tools and Sample Files

The examples used in this appendix will be smallish and somewhat toylike because more realistic ones would be far too large to be usefully reproduced in print. Full-scale examples and other materials relevant to this book are available, however, on the World Wide Web. At the site maintained by the Linguistics Laboratory at The University of Southern Maine, readers will find all of the example spreadsheets used in the book. These include all the spreadsheet functions used to construct the examples and some templates that can be used in developing new experiments. The site also includes detailed reports on some of the experiments mentioned in the book, including listings of materials and results. The web address for the site is http://www.usm.maine.edu/~lin.

C.2 Building Questionnaires (Chapter 9)

Excel provides a concatenation function "&" that can be used to assemble text strings appearing in different cells into a single string. This can be used to assemble the various members of a token set from a list of the common components of those sentences. A formula of the form

=D4&" "&D6

concatenates the contents of cell D4 with a single blank character (denoted by " "), and concatenates that with the contents of cell D6.

This function can be used to construct a token set from a series of components, as illustrated in Figure 25. The formulas appearing in B10:B13 reflect the contents of the cells in D10:D13.

Once a single set of components (as in D4:D7 in Figure 25) and a set of formulas have been constructed, further token sets can be derived from the original example. The text components for additional token sets are entered in one or more columns to the right of Column D, with parallel components appearing on the same row as in the first token set.

When the cells D10:D13 are selected (as in Figure 26), a "fill handle" appears in the lower right corner of the selected range.

By pointing at the fill handle and dragging it directly to the right by one or more columns, all the formulas in D10:D13 are copied rightward over the range covered by the drag operation. Simultaneously (because the original formulas are implicitly defined in relative terms), each new formula is adjusted to point to cells in the same column as the formula itself. Thus the original formulas can be extended to construct many further token sets to the right of the original.

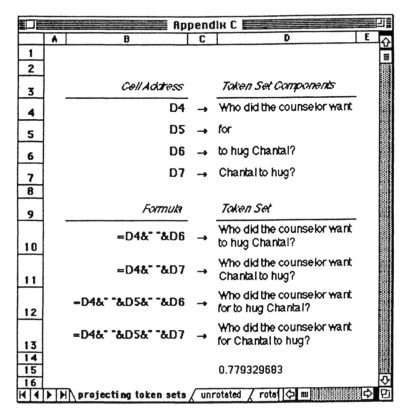

Figure 25. Formulas for assembling the sentences of a token set from a set of fixed components.

Note that there is a numeric value in cell D15. This is generated by the function =RAND( ), which should be copied to the right along with the formulas that construct the token sets. This will place a random number in the corresponding cell below each token set. Once the complete table of token sets is constructed, the full table, including the rows of sentence components, the rows of constructed token sets, and the row of random numbers, should be selected and a rowwise sort operation should be done using the row of random numbers as the sort key.[1] This randomizes the sequence of token sets from left to right to eliminate any trends or patterns that might have affected particular subsequences of token sets within the larger set.

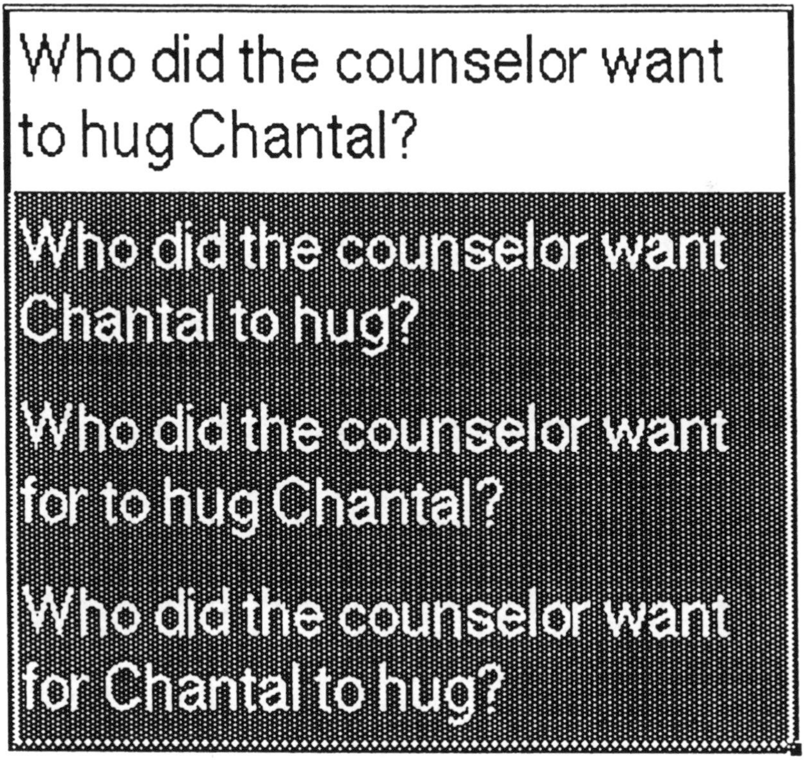

Figure 26. Selected range with fill handle in the lower right corner.

After this sort operation, the random numbers can be replaced by permanent Item ID numbers or codes.

The complete table of token sets and their ID numbers should next be copied into a new blank worksheet (preferably in the same workbook). This copy operation should also accomplish two further effects. First, the table of token sets should be copied as "values" (not formulas) and the rows and columns should be transposed (see the Edit/Paste Special command).[2] This should provide a table in the new worksheet that has as many columns as there are different sentences within each token set, plus a column for the ID numbers and as many rows as there are token sets. The sentences should appear in the cells as plain text. A schematic representation of this list appears in Figure 27.

	A	B	C	D	E	F	G
1							
2		S1	NTSE(1)	NTOE(1)	WTSE(1)	WTOE(1)	
3		S2	NTSE(2)	NTOE(2)	WTSE(2)	WTOE(2)	
4		S3	NTSE(3)	NTOE(3)	WTSE(3)	WTOE(3)	
5		S4	NTSE(4)	NTOE(4)	WTSE(4)	WTOE(4)	
6		S5	NTSE(5)	NTOE(5)	WTSE(5)	WTOE(5)	
7		S6	NTSE(6)	NTOE(6)	WTSE(6)	WTOE(6)	
8		S7	NTSE(7)	NTOE(7)	WTSE(7)	WTOE(7)	
9		S8	NTSE(8)	NTOE(8)	WTSE(8)	WTOE(8)	
10		S9	NTSE(9)	NTOE(9)	WTSE(9)	WTOE(9)	
11		S10	NTSE(10)	NTOE(10)	WTSE(10)	WTOE(10)	
12		S11	NTSE(11)	NTOE(11)	WTSE(11)	WTOE(11)	
13		S12	NTSE(12)	NTOE(12)	WTSE(12)	WTOE(12)	
14							

Appendix C

unrotated / rotating 1 /

Figure 27. Schematic of a list of "that"-trace token sets.

NOTE: The worksheet shows 12 token sets (S1 . . . S12), each of which includes sentences of four different types, with each sentence being represented here by symbols for its type and token set number, such as NTSE(3) or WTOE(7). Note that all of the sentences of any one type appear in the same column.

The goal of the next operation is to replicate the structure of Table 12, a set of four preliminary scripts. In effect, what's needed is to "rotate" the table seen in Figure 27 to place equal numbers of sentences of the four types in each of the four columns of sentences.

This is achieved by shifting blocks of sentences from the right side of the table to the left via Excel's drag and drop feature. The operation is applied first to the three WTOE sentences for Token Sets 4-6 that appear in the range F5:F7 at the right margin of the table in Figure 27. The block of cells is selected (see Figure 28), the SHIFT key is depressed, the cursor is pointed at the boundary around the selected block of cells, and the mouse button depressed. Keeping the mouse button depressed, the cursor is then moved to the left edge of the range C5:C7. When the cursor is pointing at somewhere close to the middle of the left edge of this range, a large gray I-beam cursor will appear at the boundary of Columns B and C and indicate the point where the block of cells will move to. When the mouse button is released, the selected block of cells is moved to the indicated location and all the cells lying between its old and new positions are shifted to the right.

S3	NTSE(3)	NTOE(3)	WTSE(3)	WTOE(3)
S4	NTSE(4)	NTOE(4)	WTSE(4)	WTOE(4)
S5	NTSE(5)	NTOE(5)	WTSE(5)	WTOE(5)
S6	NTSE(6)	NTOE(6)	WTSE(6)	WTOE(6)
S7	NTSE(7)	NTOE(7)	WTSE(7)	WTOE(7)

Figure 28. Selecting a block of cells.

	A	B	C	D	E	F	G
1							
2		S1	NTSE(1)	NTOE(1)	WTSE(1)	WTOE(1)	
3		S2	NTSE(2)	NTOE(2)	WTSE(2)	WTOE(2)	
4		S3	NTSE(3)	NTOE(3)	WTSE(3)	WTOE(3)	
5		S4	NTSE(4)	NTOE(4)	WTSE(4)	WTOE(4)	
6		S5	NTSE(5)	NTOE(5)	WTSE(5)	WTOE(5)	
7		S6	NTSE(6)	NTOE(6)	WTSE(6)	WTOE(6)	
8		S7	NTSE(7)	NTOE(7)	WTSE(7)	WTOE(7)	
9		S8	NTSE(8)	NTOE(8)	WTSE(8)	WTOE(8)	
10		S9	NTSE(9)	NTOE(9)	WTSE(9)	WTOE(9)	
11		S10	NTSE(10)	NTOE(10)	WTSE(10)	WTOE(10)	
12		S11	NTSE(11)	NTOE(11)	WTSE(11)	WTOE(11)	
13		S12	NTSE(12)	NTOE(12)	WTSE(12)	WTOE(12)	
14							

unrotated \ **rotating** / rotated

Figure 29. "Rotating" a list of token sets.

The same operation is next applied to the range E8:F10 that contains the WTSE and WTOE blocks of sentences for Token Sets 7-9, and then to range D11:F13 containing the NTOE, WTSE, and WTOE blocks for Token Sets 10-12. The complete process is summarized in Figure 29.

Once this operation is complete, the structure of Table 12 should be achieved, as in Figure 30.

The next series of operations applies the process described in Table 13 in Chapter 9 to each of the four preliminary scripts in Figure 30. The aim of this effort is to integrate each preliminary script with the list of filler sentences and to construct an appropriate semirandom ordering of the full list of experimental and filler materials. This

	A	B	C	D	E	F	G
				Preliminary Scripts			
1			1	2	3	4	
2		S1	NTSE(1)	NTOE(1)	WTSE(1)	WTOE(1)	
3		S2	NTSE(2)	NTOE(2)	WTSE(2)	WTOE(2)	
4		S3	NTSE(3)	NTOE(3)	WTSE(3)	WTOE(3)	
5		S4	WTOE(4)	NTSE(4)	NTOE(4)	WTSE(4)	
6		S5	WTOE(5)	NTSE(5)	NTOE(5)	WTSE(5)	
7		S6	WTOE(6)	NTSE(6)	NTOE(6)	WTSE(6)	
8		S7	WTSE(7)	WTOE(7)	NTSE(7)	NTOE(7)	
9		S8	WTSE(8)	WTOE(8)	NTSE(8)	NTOE(8)	
10		S9	WTSE(9)	WTOE(9)	NTSE(9)	NTOE(9)	
11		S10	NTOE(10)	WTSE(10)	WTOE(10)	NTSE(10)	
12		S11	NTOE(11)	WTSE(11)	WTOE(11)	NTSE(11)	
13		S12	NTOE(12)	WTSE(12)	WTOE(12)	NTSE(12)	
14							

Appendix C — rotated / Sheet3 / Sheet4

Figure 30. Same structure as Table 12 (a counterbalanced set of four preliminary scripts).

operation must be applied to each preliminary script to produce a list that we will term simply a *script*. Each script should be used in two or more different orderings. Table 16 includes a summary of the key concepts connected with scripts.

Although this process may appear tedious at first glance, it takes an experienced user less than 2 minutes to apply all of the following procedures to generate one ordering of one script. Because only six to eight ordered scripts are needed for most experiments, the total time investment in this process per experiment is not large (once the investigator is familiar with the tools and the process itself).

Each pass through the four-step process described in Table 13 produces one unique ordering for one script.

The Table 13 process starts with the construction of a template like that schematized in Figure 31. The template consists of a repeating series of "Block IDs," a column of blank cells for Item IDs, a column of blank cells into which experimental and filler sentence lists can be copied, and a column of random numbers. There should be as many distinct Block IDs used in the left-hand column as there are to be blocks in the final ordered scripts. However many Block IDs there

Table 16 Key concepts related to scripts and their structure and ordering.

Script	Each script consists of a unique subset of all the experimental sentences in the full list of token sets. Each script has exactly one sentence from each token set, includes representatives of all the available sentence types, and has equal numbers of each of the several types. There are as many scripts as there are different sentences in one token set.
Ordered Script	Each ordered script is a unique sequencing of all the materials in the script; each script should appear in two or more orderings. Each ordering of a script is broken into a number of subsections termed *blocks*, the number of blocks being the integer result of dividing the total number of token sets by the number of sentence types within each token set.
Block	Each block includes one representative of each of the sentence types and a number of filler sentences (the number being the integer result of dividing total number of filler sentences by the number of blocks). Within each block, items appear in semirandom order.
Semirandom	The order of appearance of the sentences within one block is subject to a controlled randomization process. The process of constructing the sequence within the block is random, but only those sequences are used where no more than two experimental sentences (i.e., those drawn from the token sets) appear consecutively.

are, there should be a repeating series of them down the column. The number of repetitions of this series is equal to the total number of experimental and filler sentences that will appear in each block. The RAND( ) function can be used to generate the column of random numbers. Once an appropriate template is constructed for a particular experiment, the template should be saved so that copies of it can be generated for each new script and ordering needed for the full experiment. Excel provides a template file type in the File/Save As dialogue. When a worksheet is saved in this format, each time the template file is opened, Excel creates a new workbook with a unique name.

To construct one ordering of one script, the list of experimental sentences from one preliminary script (see Figure 30) is copied into the upper part of the sentence column in the template and the list of fillers (usually constant for all scripts and orderings in one experiment) is copied into the lower part of the column. At the same time, the Item IDs should be copied into the Item ID column. Notice that the Item IDs in the schematic example in Figure 32 indicate that the sentence is an experimental item (the initial "S"), show the ID number

	A	B	C	D	E	F
		Block ID	Item ID	Sentence	Random Number	
1						
2		1	-	....	0.760010	
3		2	-	....	0.158528	
4		3	-	....	0.706782	
5		1	-	....	0.772257	
6		2	-	....	0.239562	
7		3	-	....	0.551109	
8		1	-	....	0.206695	
9		2	-	....	0.648457	
10		3	-	....	0.952483	
11		1	-	....	0.111553	
12		2	-	....	0.546889	
13		3	-	....	0.303434	
14		1	-	....	0.515593	
15		2	-	....	0.561069	
16		3	-	....	0.133546	
17		1	-	....	0.738032	
18		2	-	....	0.139082	
19		3	-	....	0.764607	
20		1	-	....	0.468580	
21		2	-	....	0.231173	
22		3	-	....	0.854345	
23		1	-	....	0.416409	
24		2	-	....	0.609614	
25		3	-	....	0.427696	
26						

Appendix C — template / template +

Figure 31. A template for executing the process described in Table 12.

of the token set, and indicate which particular condition this sentence represents ("NS" for No "that," Subject Extraction, "WO" for With "that," Object Extraction, and so on). Here the IDs for filler sentences indicate only that the sentence is a filler and give its number. Sometimes further distinctions among filler types will also need to be encoded.

Once the preliminary script and filler list are entered in a template, only three sort operations remain to complete this ordering of the current script. Each of these sort operations can be completed very quickly by selecting the relevant range (starting from the column that holds the data that will control the sort operation) and clicking on Excel's Sort Ascending button:

```
┌──────────────────────────────────────────────────────────┐
│ ≣⊡════════════════ Appendix C ═══════════════ ⊡≣          │
├────┬───┬───┬────┬──────────────┬──────────┬───┬──────────┤
│    │ A │ B │ C  │      D       │    E     │ F │          │
├────┼───┼───┼────┼──────────────┼──────────┼───┤          │
│    │   │Block│Item│              │ Random   │   │          │
│    │   │ ID │ ID │   Sentence   │ Number   │   │          │
│  1 │   │   │    │              │          │   │          │
│  2 │   │ 1 │S1_NS│Who did Nona es...│0.055481│   │          │
│  3 │   │ 2 │S2_NS│Who are the stu...│0.259332│   │          │
│  4 │   │ 3 │S3_NS│Who did the det...│0.179296│   │          │
│  5 │   │ 1 │S4_WO│Who does the nu...│0.019341│   │          │
│  6 │   │ 2 │S5_WO│Who does she th...│0.813805│   │          │
│  7 │   │ 3 │S6_WO│Who had the peo...│0.157172│   │          │
│  8 │   │ 1 │S7_WS│Who might Emily...│0.732924│   │          │
│  9 │   │ 2 │S8_WS│Who did they cl...│0.801952│   │          │
│ 10 │   │ 3 │S9_WS│Who did the edi...│0.591400│   │          │
│ 11 │   │ 1 │S10_NO│Who does Lou ex...│0.114735│  │          │
│ 12 │   │ 2 │S11_NO│Who did the cou...│0.346352│  │          │
│ 13 │   │ 3 │S12_NO│Who does your m...│0.890398│  │          │
│ 14 │   │ 1 │F1  │External jacks...│0.078323│   │          │
│ 15 │   │ 2 │F2  │Matters improv...│0.916413│   │          │
│ 16 │   │ 3 │F3  │Who the presen...│0.999352│   │          │
│ 17 │   │ 1 │F4  │Ironically, re...│0.249058│   │          │
│ 18 │   │ 2 │F5  │Solution Peter...│0.456042│   │          │
│ 19 │   │ 3 │F6  │The also expan...│0.844186│   │          │
│ 20 │   │ 1 │F7  │Who must also ...│0.301013│   │          │
│ 21 │   │ 2 │F8  │The absolute t...│0.496661│   │          │
│ 22 │   │ 3 │F9  │Who does Darle...│0.416967│   │          │
│ 23 │   │ 1 │F10 │NAFTA was a bo...│0.962412│   │          │
│ 24 │   │ 2 │F11 │Who worshipped...│0.653221│   │          │
│ 25 │   │ 3 │F12 │Who for all at...│0.211123│   │          │
│ 26 │   │   │    │              │          │   │          │
├────┴───┴───┴────┴──────────────┴──────────┴───┤          │
│ ◄◄ ◄ ► ►◄\ projecting token sets / unrd        │          │
└──────────────────────────────────────────────────────────┘
```

Figure 32. Template with sentences.

The three sort operations have the effects of (a) randomly assigning sentences to blocks, (b) segregating the blocks, and (c) randomly ordering materials within each block. For the sample data in Figure 32, these operations take the following form:

• To assign sentences to blocks, select E2:C13 (start the select operation from cell E2 and do *not* include Column B in the range to be sorted) and click Sort Ascending. Repeat this operation for the filler sentences by selecting and sorting the range E14:C25.

• To segregate the blocks, select B2:D25 (starting from B2) and click Sort Ascending.

• To randomize the order of items within each block, select the block (starting from Column D) and sort. For the first block in Figure 32, select E2:C9 and sort. For the second and third blocks, sort the ranges E10:C17 and E18:C25. Each of these sort operations should be checked to ensure that it does not create sequences of more than two consecutive experimental items. When such sequences arise, the easiest way to remove them is to re-sort the block. After each sort operation, the sorted range stays selected and all the random numbers change[3]; thus, to generate a new random ordering of the range, it is only necessary to click the Sort Ascending button again.

For a template of fixed structure that may be reused in further experiments, it is easy to automate much of the process described above by way of Excel's Visual Basic macro language. Note that, where appropriate, filler sentences can be incorporated in the template because they usually do not vary from script to script within one experiment. Where macro functions and filler sentences are built into a template, the process of generating a new ordering of a script can be executed in much less than a minute.

Once an ordering of a script is complete, the list of sentences *and their Item IDs* should be copied to a master worksheet that will ultimately contain all the orderings of all the scripts used in the experiment. The Item IDs will later be extracted to guide the decoding of data files. Each ordered script should be assigned an identifier as it is copied into the master list and the association between the identifier and the ordered script should be carefully maintained in all further operations.

A complete set of questionnaires can now be constructed by copying each ordered script into a copy of a master questionnaire. The master questionnaire should include all the invariant material that is to be presented to every informant at the beginning or end of the procedure. When the sentence list for an ordered script is copied into a questionnaire, the items can be automatically numbered by a variety of devices. If the sentence list for an ordered script is copied into a Microsoft Word file as unformatted text, each sentence will be automatically treated as a "paragraph" in Word. The list of paragraphs (sentences) in the Word document can be selected and assigned a numbering scheme en masse automatically via the Insert/Bullets and Numbering dialogue.

Because the various questionnaires for an experiment will be very similar in appearance, it is worthwhile to add identifying information to each questionnaire file to help ensure the integrity of the final printed questionnaires. Each questionnaire file should be given a unique file name that reflects or incorporates the identifier for the ordered script it contains. Each page of a questionnaire can include this file name and a time/date stamp in a header or footer that is automatically updated each time the document is printed.[4] This ensures that each time a modified questionnaire file is printed, all the pages of that printing will carry unique identifying information.

C.3 Coding/Decoding Data (Chapter 10)

The goal of the next series of steps is to convert a results file produced by a scanning system into an orderly data file patterned along the lines of Figure 23 in Chapter 10.

The tools needed to clean up and align raw data files (see Figure 16 and Figure 17) are mostly commonplace word processing functions. The task is facilitated if the files are displayed in a monospace font (e.g., Courier) so that the nth character on each line falls at the same horizontal position on each line. It is also often helpful to set the word processor or editor's display so that it displays an overt marker for space characters and nonprinting characters such as hard return or line feed (see Word's Show/Hide [¶] button). Novices should be aware of the distinction between the proprietary formats that most word processors use to store formatted word processing files and the so-called text or ASCII files. Text files are generally easier to copy or load into a spreadsheet than are files coded in one of the proprietary word processing formats, although most spreadsheets have conversion functions that accommodate a variety of input formats.

On most systems, cleaned data files in text format can be moved into a spreadsheet by way of a Copy and Paste operation originating with the editor or word processing program. Text files can also be saved and opened directly by the spreadsheet program. In this case, Excel will launch its parsing function automatically as part of the process of loading the file.

In general, the Copy-Paste route is more convenient. The copied data will appear in a single column of cells in the spreadsheet, with all the data (up to 256 characters) from each line in one cell. This column of cells should be formatted so that the contents are displayed in Courier or another monospace font (in Excel, use Format/Cells/Font). Select the single column range of cells where the copied data appear and invoke Excel's parsing function (Data/Text to Columns). This will launch a "wizard" (a series of dialogue boxes) that will guide the user through the process of specifying how the input material is to be parsed. The first dialogue box asks the user to specify whether the different fields (data items) in each row are to be distinguished by their linear position (the Fixed Width option) or by marker characters such as commas or tabs appearing between the fields (the Delimited option). In Figure 17, the first two fields (columns of data) on most lines could be distinguished either way because spaces follow the single character Type field and the seven-character ID number. However, there are no marker characters between the 37 single-character response items that appear to the right of each line (which is typical of many scanning systems). Each character represents a single informant response. The Fixed Width option must be used to parse data formatted like this.

The second dialogue box in the Text to Columns Wizard allows the user to explicitly specify where the lines are to be parsed. In the third dialogue box, the user indicates what format is to be applied to each data item recovered by way of the parsing operation, and where the array of cells that results from the parsing operation is to be placed.

The parsed data should be labeled so that each column in the data table has a label on the first row (e.g., Row 2 in Figure 18). Some of these labels can usually be generated automatically. For example, if "S1" is typed into a single cell, the cell can be selected and its fill handle dragged right across the cell's row or down along the cell's column. In either case, this will yield a series of labels in successive cells of the form "S2," "S3," and so on. This works when the string in the initial cell begins with an alphanumeric sequence of any length (up to the limit of cell capacity) and ends with an integer value having not more than 10 digits.

Once the input data (from whatever source) has been parsed, ordered, and labeled, the worksheet containing the data should be saved and backed up. Only copies of these data should be used in further analyses. The parsed and labeled data table should be preserved as is.

The next step in analyzing the data is to isolate and reformat the Item ID information that was saved with the ordered scripts so that it can be used to identify individual responses in informant data. Rows 3 through 10 in Figure 33 (the section labeled "Codes") contain reformatted Item IDs. The first of each pair of rows identifies the type of each item ("F" for filler sentences, "NO" for No "that," Object Extraction, and so on) in an ordered script. The second row of each pair of lines shows the item number (within the relevant type). Thus "WO" and "10" in Column E is a reference to Token Set 10 in the With "that," Object Extraction condition. "F" and "12" in Column F is a reference to filler sentence 12. The left-to-right order of the codes in each of the four pairs of Item ID lines corresponds to the sequence of sentences in the relevant ordered script. When large sets of labels are being constructed, the same parsing functions used earlier to put scanned data into columns can be applied here. Excel's text functions (e.g., LEFT or MID) are often also useful in constructing labels.

The most efficient way to integrate the Item ID information with the response data is to sort the full table in Figure 33 by Script ID and Line Type (see Note 1). This sort must be specified via the Data/Sort dialogue. If Script ID in Column B is specified as the Sort By column, and the Line Type column, Column C, is specified as the Then By column, Excel will group all of the lines relevant to ordered script 1 together and then sort among these lines according to the values in the Line Type column. Because all of the response data lines have been assigned a Line Type value of 3, and the two kinds of Item ID lines have values of 0 and 1, the Item ID lines will be sorted ahead of the data lines to which they are relevant, giving a table such as that in Figure 34.

To order items by number (i.e., Item ID) along each row (as in Figure 20), it is necessary to do rowwise sort operations that are governed by the Item Number values, for example, in Row 5 of Figure 20. In a table structured similarly to Figure 34, the needed sorting can be done as follows, with the four rows related to Ordered Script 1 (Rows 4 through 7) used to illustrate the process. First, the entire relevant range for a given ordered script (E4:AB7 in this case) is selected and the Data/Sort function is invoked. Clicking the Options button brings up the Sort Options dialogue, where the user should check the "Sort Left to Right" button and click OK. The Sort operation is then specified by selecting Row 4 as the Sort By field and

	A	B	C	D	E	F	G	H	I	J	K	L	AB	AC	AD
1															
2		Script ID	Line Type												
3		1	0		WO	F	NS	F	F	F	NS	NO	F		
4		1	1		10	12	1	1	9	4	2	5	5		
5		2	0		F	WS	WO	F	F	F	NO	NS	NS	C	
6		2	1		4	4	9	5	11	3	3	11	10	O	
7		3	0		F	NO	WO	F	WS	F	F	WS	NS	D	
8		3	1		6	12	4	5	3	8	3	1	7	E	
9		4	0		F	NO	NS	F	NO	F	NO	F	WS	S	
10		4	1		3	8	6	2	9	6	7	11	10		
11															
12															
13		S_ID	LT		S1	S2	S3	S4	S5	S6	S7	S8	S24		
14		1	3		4	4	8	8	7	6	2	8	3		
15		1	3		1	1	8	0	7	0	1	5	6	D	
16		2	3		3	1	0	1	7	5	8	4	7	A	
17		2	3		4	5	8	7	5	3	2	6	7	T	
18		3	3		8	8	7	8	8	7	2	2	4	A	
19		3	3		6	9	7	7	0	3	5	5	3		
20		4	3		0	2	4	3	6	9	8	8	2		
21		4	3		5	4	5	0	1	4	6	9	1		
22															

ItemIDs / Interleaved ItemIDs / Sheet4

Figure 33. Item IDs formatted for use in decoding data.

NOTE: The "Script ID" column associates each line with an ordered script in this experiment. Thus the two lines in the data range (B14:AB21) with Script IDs of 2 represent data from informants who used ordered script 2, and the two lines in the Codes range (B3:AB10) with Script IDs of 2 are the Item IDs that identify the type and number of each of the responses from informants. Columns M through AA have been hidden.

specifying a Descending sort on this field (this will put the fillers, marked "F," after the experimentals). The No Header Row button should also be checked. The Sort operation is then executed. This produces an order in which all items of the same type (i.e., all the "WO" items, all the "F" items, and so on) appear together left to right. In this case (because of the descending sort), all the various categories of experimental sentences will appear first in alphabetical order by type ID, then the filler sentences. At this point, the range representing Ordered Script 1 should be seen as divided into two parts, a section with data from experimental sentences and a section with data on

Script ID	Line Type	S1	S2	S3	S4	S5	S6	S7	S8	S24
1	0	WO	F	NS	F	F	F	NS	NO	F
1	1	10	12	1	1	9	4	2	5	5
1	3	4	4	8	8	7	6	2	8	3
1	3	1	1	8	0	7	0	1	5	6
2	0	F	WS	WO	F	F	F	NO	NS	NS
2	1	4	4	9	5	11	3	3	11	10
2	3	3	1	0	1	7	5	8	4	7
2	3	4	5	8	7	5	3	2	6	7
3	0	F	NO	WO	F	WS	F	F	WS	NS
3	1	6	12	4	5	3	8	3	1	7
3	3	8	8	7	8	8	7	2	2	4
3	3	6	9	7	7	0	3	5	5	3
4	0	F	NO	NS	F	NO	F	NO	F	WS
4	1	3	8	6	2	9	6	7	11	10
4	3	0	2	4	3	6	9	8	8	2
4	3	5	4	5	0	1	4	6	9	1

Figure 34. Item IDs interleaved with data rows.

NOTE: Columns M through AA have again been hidden to save space. Note that no columns or rows should be hidden in ranges selected for use in a sort operation.

filler sentences. Two further sort operations, one for fillers and one for experimentals, will achieve the intended result (as in Figure 20). In each case, the same range is selected as in the previous sort, except that it is limited to only the filler or experimental sentences. The sort function is invoked and directed to do the sort using only the Item Number row, Row 5 in Figure 34. When this operation has been applied to fillers and experimental sentences, the items will appear left to right in numerical order within each type. The same sequence of sorting operations is then applied to the blocks of data for other ordered scripts.

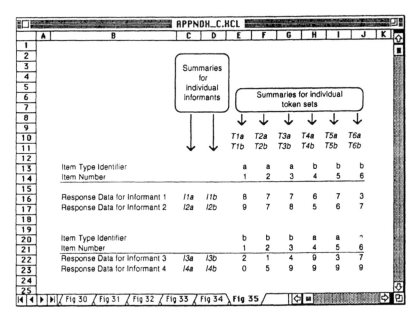

Figure 35. A small data table.

C.4 Summarizing Data (Chapter 11)

The procedures described in this section add new columns and rows to tables structured along the lines of Figure 20. For convenience, the essential structure of Figure 20 will be represented here by the small data table shown in Figure 35, which adds two columns in which to summarize the data for individual informants and two rows in which to summarize the data for individual token sets.

This table represents a hypothetical experiment in which four informants judged each of six token sets (and where each token set included sentences of two types, denoted *a* and *b*). This section will identify the Excel functions needed to construct the several different kinds of mathematical summary discussed in Chapter 11, and show how these functions can be applied to both summaries by informants and by token sets. There are convenience features in Excel that can facilitate the operations described here, but the current discussion will focus mainly on Excel's mathematical functions rather than the mechanics of entering them into the worksheet.

Each of the cells marked by placeholders in the summary tables (e.g., *I1a, T2b*) in Figure 35 must be replaced by an Excel formula that provides the appropriate summary of the relevant range within the relevant column.

Means Summaries

To generate a summary using means, each placeholder in the range C16:C23 is replaced by the mean of that informant's responses to Type *a* sentences. These means are generated by a formula of the form:

=AVERAGE(E16:G16)

The first of these formulas can be constructed by typing in all the material up to the "(" and then selecting the target range with the mouse. Excel will enter the range reference in the formula. The finished formula can then be copied and pasted into the cell below (containing place-holder *I2a*) to generate the appropriate summaries for Type *a* sentences on those rows. The same formula can also be copied over placeholders *I3a*, *I4a* (which will generate summaries for Type *b* sentences, instead of Type *a*). A later operation will get these values (and others in the token set summaries) into the appropriate column.

The process can be repeated for the column of cells summarizing responses on the Type *b* sentences.

Summaries by token set are constructed in essentially the same fashion. In the cell occupied by placeholder *T1a*, the AVERAGE formula is entered up through the "(". Then the range E16:E17 is selected with the mouse. The formula can be completed by typing ")" and RETURN, or just RETURN (Excel can supply the final ")" for most simple formulas). The formula entered for placeholder *T1a* can then be replicated by selecting its cell and dragging the fill handle rightward to highlight the cell containing *T6a*. and all the intervening cells. This replicates the formula so that each copy summarizes responses in its own column. The process can be repeated for the second row of placeholders.

The last step of the operation is to take account of the fact that the formula entered for *I1a* actually summarizes responses to Type *b* sentences for Informants 3 and 4, and that the formula for *T1a* summarizes Type *b* responses for Token Sets 4, 5, and 6. Once the complete table of summary formulas is constructed, values are rearranged by an application of the cell drag and drop feature exploited above in connection with the table of preliminary scripts in Figure 30. The *I3a* and *I4a* cells (C22:C23) are highlighted, the SHIFT key is depressed, and the selected range is dragged to the right of Column D (whose contents on these rows now moves into Column C). In their new location, the formulas still point to the same ranges they did before they were moved. Now all the summaries in Column C are for Type *a* sentences and all those in Column D are for Type *b* items. The same process is applied to the right half of the two rows of summaries by token set. The positions of the first and second rows are exchanged.

This same general process for building formulas and constructing summary tables is applied in constructing the other types of summaries discussed below. Different summary types can be constructed in new columns and rows parallel to the summary ranges shown in Figure 35, or the original data table can be reproduced in a new worksheet and the new summaries constructed there.

Percentage Summaries

Percentage summaries can be constructed by way of two variants of Excel's counting function. The COUNT function counts the number of numeric values that appear in the indicated range. COUNTIF counts the number of numbers in the indicated range that satisfy some criterion (e.g., ">1"). These can be combined to determine the percentage of values in a range that meet a criterion. If the formula

=COUNTIF(E16:G16,">=8")/COUNT(E16:G16)

replaces the placeholder *I1a*, Figure 35 Excel will return a result of .33, the proportion of responses in the indicated range that are at or above 8.

Standard Scores

To calculate standard scores, it is generally best to first calculate a mean and standard deviation for each informant (or token set), although this is not necessary. At the cost of some redundancy, the mean and standard deviation calculations can also be built into the formulas that calculate standard scores. I will assume that the mean and standard deviation are to be calculated separately because these are often needed in other processes.

The overall mean and standard deviation for Informant 1 in Figure 35 can be calculated via these formulas:

```
=AVERAGE(E16:J16)
=STDEV(E16:J16)
```

I will assume that these values are entered in columns to the right of the table of responses in Figure 35 (in Columns K and L). With these values in place, the standardized means for Type *a* and *b* sentences can be calculated with the following formula:

```
=STANDARDIZE(AVERAGE(E16:G16),K16,L16)
```

Geometric Means

Geometric means can be calculated for token sets by way of the same procedures as those described above. For placeholder *T1a*, the formula takes the following form:

```
=GEOMEAN(E16:E17)
```

C.5 Transferring Data to a Statistical Program

Worksheets containing summary tables should be carefully preserved. Data can be passed to statistical software in a variety of ways. A copy of the summary worksheet can be converted to values (i.e., all the formulas can be replaced by the then-current results of those formulas) and superfluous material removed (e.g., columns containing individual responses). The resulting summary worksheet can be saved as a new worksheet (some statistical software can read some spreadsheet file formats directly), or it can be converted to text or other file formats (Excel offers many options under the File Type selector in the File/Save As dialogue). It is often also possible to use copy and paste operations to move data into statistical software.

Notes

1. A general caution about SORT operations is in order. Be very careful to always include all the columns and rows that are relevant to a particular table in each sort operation. Inspect the results of any sort carefully before executing any other operations. When the range to be sorted is not properly defined, sort operations can be quite destructive. Excel provides a powerful UNDO feature that allows the user to

back out of most sort operations that go wrong, but this is most effective if it is used immediately after the error is made.

2. The transpose operation can be avoided if desired by applying the same logic for constructing token sets as described earlier on a vertical rather than horizontal axis. The column of sentence components and formulas in Figure 25 can instead be laid out along a single row. Components for new token sets are then constructed in succeeding rows and the formulas copied downward instead of rightward. This process will save the transposition step later on but may not be practicable unless the investigator has access to a relatively large monitor.

3. The random numbers are generated by the RAND( ) function, which automatically yields a new random number in each cell where it is used each time a sort is performed (provided Excel is set for automatic recalculation).

4. In Word, the name of the current file is invoked by way of the field code FILENAME.

Appendix D:
Token Set Data From a "That"-Trace Experiment

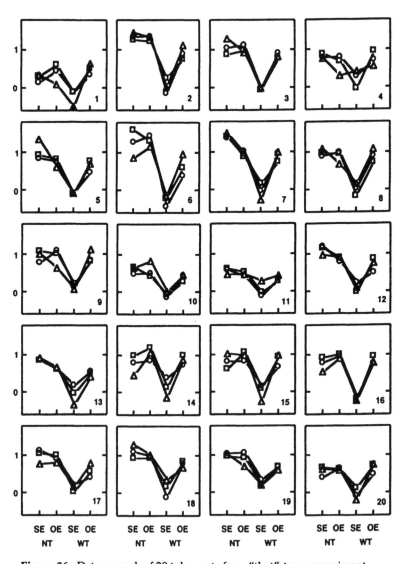

SE OE SE OE   SE OE SE OE   SE OE SE OE   SE OE SE OE
   NT   WT   NT   WT   NT   WT   NT   WT

Figure 36. Data on each of 20 token sets for a "that"-trace experiment.

NOTE: Each graph summarizes the data for 1 of the 20 token sets listed in Table 17. On each line in each graph, the data points represent the No "that"/Subject Extraction, No "that"/Object Extraction, With "that"/Subject Extraction, and With "that"/Object Extraction conditions in that order, left to right. Each line represents data collected at a different site (◆ Wayne State College, Nebraska, N = 192; ■ University of Alabama at Birmingham, N = 33; ▲ University of Southern Maine, N = 107). Because each data point summarizes responses to a single sentence, only about one quarter of each sample contributed to any one data point. Thus the number of informants contributing to each data point varies from around 8 to 48, for the Alabama and Nebraska samples, respectively.

Table 17 Token sets.

Item Number	Sentence
1	Who was the nurse imagining (that) would find her? /(that) she would find?
2	Who do you suppose (that) invited Ann to the circus? /(that) Ann invited to the circus?
3	Who did Marie hope (that) would dance with Phil? /(that) Phil would dance with?
4	Who will Jim announce (that) is running against him? /(that) he is running against?
5	Who does he expect (that) will visit the neighbors? /(that) the neighbors will visit?
6	Who do you think (that) likes John? /(that) John likes?
7	Who do you feel (that) should take care of Fred? /(that) Fred should take care of?
8	Who did Jane suspect (that) had kidnapped Fred? /(that) Fred had kidnapped?
9	Who did the operator say (that) called Maxwell on the car-phone? /(that) Maxwell called on the car-phone?
10	Who did the actor pretend (that) had killed the soldier? /(that) the soldier had killed?
11	Who had the lawyer heard (that) would be fighting for the defendant? /(that) the defendant would be fighting for?
12	Who are they assuming (that) helped Chris with the taxes? /(that) Chris helped with the taxes?
13	Who did the horse owners bet (that) would beat Secretariat in the contest? /(that) Secretariat would beat in the contest?
14	Who will Dan insist (that) is in love with him? /(that) he is in love with?
15	Who did the article proclaim (that) was attacking the criminal? /(that) the criminal was attacking?
16	Who did the kids wish (that) could go swimming with them? /(that) they could go swimming with?
17	Who does the teacher believe (that) hurt the boy? /(that) the boy hurt?
18	Who did they presume (that) had rescued Bill? /that) Bill had rescued?
19	Who did she claim (that) beat up the boy? /(that) the boy beat up?
20	Who had you dreamed (that) would marry John? /(that) John would marry?

NOTE: The table lists the 20 token sets used in the "that"-trace experiment described in Figure 36.

Appendix E: Sample Questionnaire for Scannable Line Drawing

Sentence Judgment Experiment

The experiment you are participating in is part of a pilot project on sentence acceptability funded by the (U.S.) National Science Foundation. If you would like more information about the project, we will be happy to tell you more about the goals of the work and the results we've achieved so far. You may get in touch with us at the address shown below.

We very much appreciate your willingness to assist us in this work.

None of the information collected here will be associated with your name in any way.

DO NOT WRITE YOUR NAME ON THIS QUESTIONNAIRE OR THE ANSWER SHEET.

Wayne Cowart
Principal Investigator

Dana McDaniel
Co-Principal Investigator

Language Sciences Laboratory
University of Southern Maine
96 Falmouth St.
Portland, ME 04103

(207) 780-4477

E-mail: cowart@usm.maine.edu

Subject ID   9999

Preliminaries

You should have received a #2 pencil and a green (General Purpose - NCS) Answer Sheet with this questionnaire. Please let the experimenter know if you are missing either of these items.

The following pages in this questionnaire will teach you how to record your responses in this experiment. It is extremely important that you read the instructions carefully and do all the tasks specified. ALL OF THE STEPS OF THIS PROCEDURE ARE IMPORTANT. SKIP NOTHING!!!

If at any point you are unclear about anything you are asked to do, please feel free to ask the experimenter for clarification.

Home Town

All other responses you make in this procedure will be recorded on the green Answer Sheet. However, your response to this item is to be recorded here on the questionnaire.

Question: Where did you begin grade school (first grade)? (Please write your responses to this question in the blanks provided below)

CITY/TOWN _____

STATE OR COUNTRY _____

Other Demographic Information

Please take out your green Answer Sheet now and use it to record the next several responses. Please use your #2 pencil for this and make heavy, clear marks, as shown below. Make no stray marks on the Answer Sheet.

	A B C D E F G H I J		A B C D E F G H I J
Make marks like this 1	O O O ◆ O O O O O O	not this 1	O O O ◐ O O O O O O

Please check to see that the red number stamped in the upper left hand corner of your Answer Sheet agrees with the Subject ID stamped in the box on the first page of this questionnaire.

In the block marked "SEX" (just left of the heavy green line in the middle of your Answer Sheet) mark the appropriate category.

There is another labeled "GRADE or EDUC" just below the box marked "SEX". Please indicate here how many years of formal schooling you have completed. In the U.S., completing high school counts as 12, and completing a bachelor's degree counts as 16.

In the block marked "BIRTH DATE" (lower left), fill in the appropriate circle for the month of your birth, then write in the day and year of your birth and fill in the appropriate circles below for the day and year.

Each of the columns A-H in the block labeled "IDENTIFICATION NUMBER" will be used for a different question. The questions are listed below. Please write in your response in the empty box at the top of each column, then fill in the appropriate bubble below. Remember: This information is not associated with your name in this study.

Column A: Are you a native speaker of American English? (0) yes (1) no

Column B: Are you a native speaker of British English? (0) yes (1) no

Column C: Are you a native speaker of another variety of English (Jamaican, Indian, Australian, etc.)? (0) yes (1) no

Column D: Among the parents/caregivers of the family you grew up with, what was the highest level of education completed by any of those individuals?
(0) high school or less
(1) college
(2) masters degree
(3) doctorate or-law or medical degree
(4) don't know

Column E: Do you ever choose to write with your left hand? (Ignore cases where you are forced by circumstances to use your left hand, as when there is temporary injury, a heavy package in your right hand, etc.)
(0)never (1) sometimes (2) always

Column F: Are any members of your immediate family (biological parents and siblings only) left handed, so far as you know?
(0) confident some are left-handed
(1)-not-sure, some could be left-handed
(2) confident all are right-handed

Column G: What is your academic major.
(0) English (1) a foreign language
(2) Linguistics (3) Other

Column H: Did you and your family move from one city or town to another while you were in grade school (Years 1-6)? (0) yes (1) no

If you answered Yes to Question H, please answer Question I as well.

Column I: If you moved, how long did you continue school in the city/town where you began first grade?
(0) less than on year
(1)-one-to-two-years
(2)-three-to-four-years
(3)-more-than-four-years

The Response Procedure

The experiment you are about to participate in uses an <u>unusual</u> response procedure. This page gives you some critical background you will need to use this procedure correctly.

Suppose you were asked to judge the relative area of these two circles.

Circle B is about three times the area of A.

One way you could report your impression of the relative sizes is to draw two lines, making the second three times longer than the first .

If we had a completely free choice, this is how we would have you report your impressions to us in this experiment. Unfortunately, we would then have to spend months measuring tens of thousands of lines.

What we will do instead is this. Each time we ask you to judge something, there will be an item like this on your Answer Sheet.

```
      A B C D E F G H I J
1 -   O O O O O O O O O O
```

But, WE WANT YOU TO THINK OF THE ROW OF DOTS, A THRU J, AS A LINE. So, if you were using this dotted line to describe Circles A and B, you should think of it like this.

The difference is that now the lines have to stop on one of the dots.

Looking at it this way, there are actually three ways that you could report that Circle B looks about three times bigger than Circle A. In addition to the one shown above, there are also these two other equally good ways of reporting the same thing.

What matters in this experiment is that you GET THE RATIOS RIGHT! You can make long lines or short ones, just so the differences in line length agree with your impressions.

One more complication: We want you to think of A thru J as a line, but WE DON'T WANT YOU TO ACTUALLY DRAW LINES. Instead, just show us where each of your lines would stop. For each item, fill in the dot that is closest to where your line would end and for that item. For example, the difference between Circles A and B could be indicated any of the following three ways.

```
      A B C D E F G H I J
A     O ● O O O O O O O O

      A B C D E F G H I J
B     O O O O O ● O O O O


      A B C D E F G H I J
A     O O ● O O O O O O O

      A B C D E F G H I J
B     O O O O O O O O ● O


      A B C D E F G H I J
A     ● O O O O O O O O O

      A B C D E F G H I J
B     O O ● O O O O O O O
```

Now for some practice.

Practice

As a warm-up for the main experiment, we'd like you to use the procedure we've just introduced to describe the circles below. The scores you assign should reflect the relative size of each circle COMPARED TO THE FIRST ONE. Use the green Answer Sheet for your responses. Find the place for Item #1 on Side 1 of the Answer Sheet. Now look at Circle #1 below and decide what score (remember – think of it as a line length) you want to use to represent the size of Circle #1. Fill in the appropriate bubble in Item #1 on the Answer Sheet. For Circle #2, select a score (line length) that shows how much larger #2 is, compared to #1. Continue on and enter scores for each of the remaining eight circles using Items 3 through 10 on the Answer Sheet.

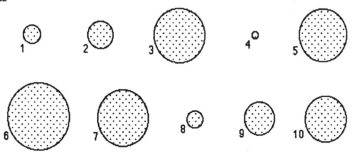

Instructions for Sentence Judgments

IMPORTANT! Do not begin this portion of the experiment until you have read the instructions on the preceding page and completed the Practice items above.

We need some information from you about your evaluation of some sentences we've listed below.

We would like you to imagine that your job is to teach English to speakers of other languages.

For each sentence listed below, we would like you to do the following. Please read the sentence, then ask yourself if the sentence seems English-sounding or not. Suppose one of your students were to use this sentence. If we ignore pronunciation, would the student sound like a native speaker? Or would the sentence seem strange or unnatural to a native speaker no matter how it was pronounced? Your task is to tell us how English-sounding each sentence is using a scale.

Let the first sentence be your reference. Assign a score for it that seems appropriate to you. Keep in mind that some of the sentences you see later may seem better or worse. Assign a score for each new sentence so that the score shows how much better or worse that sentence is compared to the first sentence. The better a sentence seems, the higher the score you should use. Once you've given a response for a sentence, please don't go back and reconsider.

We recognize that the scale is crude; it will not express some subtle differences between sentences. Just do the best you can.

You don't need to worry about grammar rules you may have studied in school. Tell us what seems most natural to you, whether or not that is 'proper' by rules you may have learned. We are only interested in your sense of what would be appropriate in ordinary relaxed conversation.

Also, please don't struggle over individual sentences. Make the best quick judgment you can for each sentence and go on to the next.

There are 92 sentences on the questionnaire, numbered from #11 to #102. Please be sure to do them all.

Please record your responses on the Answer Sheet starting with Item #11.

The Sentences

11) This is a painful movie to watch.

12) Israel's $13,000 annual per the capita income parts Western Europe.

13) We had doubted that people would drive up and wait at the border on week nights.

14) It's also quite possible to build your own shelves bookcase, especially if have got a knowledgeable friend neighbor who's willing the help.

15) Studying a the subject, we realize that Rob depended on people they being able think like.

16) Giro Sport Design Inc., based near Santa Cruz, California, are making bicycle helmets bicycle pumps in Mexico and hopes to sell them there soon.

17) 58 percent of the businesses supported an import tax to make Japanese products less competitive.

18) His brother believe they have are on the brink of a breakthrough to the really big time.

19) A most extraordinary party took place on the third floor second floor.

20) Perhaps it took an adventurer, enigmatic and reckless, without a plan, heedless of risk, a con man, to do what he did.

21) There has did no plot, no characters to identify at, no hope.

22) Women has been assigned to non-combat ships and served temporary duty aboard combat ships in the past.

23) Who the presented are with harsh, sardonic?

24) Who claimed that the resulting conflict between Serbia quickly escalated into World War I?

25) The higher the number, the faster the modem and the less it costs to use online services that charge by the hour.

26) "It's just a big problem as see it," Freeman said.

27) Who have questioned many of the basic principles of Lang's theories?

28) Who did the article proclaim that was attacking the criminal?

29) Who had you dreamed that John would marry?

30) Who do you think John likes?

31) Who, when Lisa contracted cancer found herself terrible in pain, found he was not of all sure his of theory?

32) External jacks plug of but are next at the back cover plate.

33) During the second, the Black Pottery if Longshan phase, agriculture became more.

34) The also expand significantly northwestward into, besieging Vienna.

35) Who was the nurse imagining would find her?

36) Who must also are able to trust him, and to believes he will there for you?

37) His ability to share her view is a small triumph, but one few people can claim.

38) Ironically, reform paved the way for a more radical political transformation.

39) At the beginning of the year the month, Lambert wanted only to make money, but at the end he wanted only to save his business.

40) Who does he expect will visit the neighbors?

41) Who for all at their resiliency, however, the seem stuck in a of rut in Stanleyville?

42) Who had the lawyer heard that would be fighting for the defendant?

43) Who did the actor pretend the soldier had killed?

44) What hell going?

45) Are there people students like Suzanne in that class?

46) Many have long shared a "misconception that everyone in Mexico is poor," Grijalva said.

47) Destruction are his only.

48) Who does the teacher believe that the boy hurt?

49) What it take to do the and work is a computer, a modem, and a the phone line.

...

92) The "relationship" that develops between Brian and Carol is so pathetic that it can barely be watched.

93) On Monday will ordering 60 women sailors and officers to duty aboard the aircraft carrier USS Dwight D. Eisenhower.

94) Who did the horse owners bet that would beat Secretariat in the contest?

95) Who worshipped prayed to their ancestors, a Chinese custom that still has persists?

96) Who did Marie hope would dance with Phil?

97) He is a teacher and a writer, a pipe-smoking bachelor who lives in his book-lined Oxford home with his brother.

98) The fact that Murray is be able to combine the qualities of comedy, romance and even melodrama makes very rare.

99) Apologized and fired freelance.

100) The in 14th and 15th centuries the, a heretical Christian sect, was numerous Bosnia in.

101) Who did she claim that the boy beat up?

102) Matters improve with the arrival of Claire, whose name is on the lease.

Please now tear the FIRST PAGE off of this questionnaire and return the first page and your Answer Sheet together to the experimenter. The rest of the questionnaire can be disposed of.

Thank You very much for your assistance in this work.

References

Baird, J., & Noma, E. (1978). *Fundamentals of scaling and psychophysics.* New York: John Wiley.

Bard, E. G., Robertson, D., & Sorace, A. (1996). Magnitude estimation of linguistic acceptability. *Language, 72*(1), 32-68.

Berndt, R. S., Salasoo, A., Mitchum, C. C., & Blumstein, S. (1988). The role of intonation cues in aphasic patients' performance of the grammaticality judgment task. *Brain & Language, 34*(1), 65-97.

Bever, T. G. (1974). The ascent of the specious; or, There's a lot we don't know about mirrors. In D. Cohen (Ed.), *Explaining linguistic phenomena* (pp. 173-200). Washington, DC: Hemisphere.

Bever, T., & Carroll, J. M. (1981). On some continuous properties in language. In T. Myers, J. Laver, & J. Anderson (Eds.), *The cognitive representation of speech* (pp. 225-233). Amsterdam: North-Holland.

Bley-Vroman, R. W., Felix, S. W., & Ioup, G. L. (1988). The accessibility of universal grammar in adult language learning. *Second Language Research, 4*(1), 1-32.

Bloomfield, L. (1930). Linguistics as a science. *Studies in Philology, 27,* 533-557.

Blumstein, S. E., Milberg, W. P., Dworetzky, B., Rosen, A., & Gershberg, F. (1991). Syntactic priming effects in aphasia: An investigation of local syntactic dependencies. *Brain and Language, 40,* 393-421.

Bock, J. K. (1987). Coordinating words and syntax in speech plans. In A. Ellis (Ed.), *Progress in the psychology of language* (pp. 337-390). London: Lawrence Erlbaum.

Bock, J. K. (1990). Structure in language: Creating form in talk. *American Psychologist, 45,* 1221-1236.

Boring, E. G. (1953). A history of introspection. *Psychological Bulletin, 50*(3), 169-189.

Bransford, J. D., & Franks, J. J. (1971). The abstraction of linguistic ideas. *Cognitive Psychology, 3,* 331-350.

Carden, G. (1970). A note on conflicting idiolects. *Linguistic Inquiry, 1*(3), 281-290.

Carden, G. (1973). Dialect variation in abstract syntax. In R. W. Shuy (Ed.), *Some new directions in linguistics* (pp. 1-34). Washington, DC: Georgetown University Press.

Carroll, J. M., Bever, T. G., & Pollack, C. R. (1981). The non-uniqueness of linguistic intuitions. *Language, 57,* 368-383.

Chomsky, N. (1957). *Syntactic structures.* The Hague, the Netherlands: Mouton.

Chomsky, N. (1965). *Aspects of the theory of syntax.* Cambridge: MIT Press.

Chomsky, N. (1973). Conditions on transformations. In S. Anderson & P. Kiparsky (Eds.), *A festschrift for Morris Halle* (pp. 232-286). New York: Holt, Rinehart & Winston.

Chomsky, N. (1977). On wh-movement. In P. Culicover, T. Wasow, & A. Akmajian (Eds.), *Formal syntax* (pp. 71-132). New York: Academic Press.

Chomsky, N. (1981). *Lectures on government and binding*. Dordrecht: Foris.

Chomsky, N. (1986). *Knowledge of language: Its nature, origin and use*. New York: Praeger.

Chomsky, N., & Lasnik, H. (1977). Filters and control. *Linguistic Inquiry, 8*, 425-504.

Clark, H. H. (1973). The language as fixed effect fallacy: A critique of language statistics in psychological research. *Journal of Verbal Learning and Verbal Behavior, 12*, 335-359.

Cohen, J. (1969). *Statistical power analysis for the behavioral sciences*. New York: Academic Press.

Cowart, W. (1989a). Illicit acceptability in 'picture' NPs. *Papers from the regional meetings, Chicago Linguistic Society, 25*, 27-40.

Cowart, W. (1989b). Notes on the biology of syntactic processing. *Journal of Psycholinguistic Research, 18*, 89-103.

Cowart, W. (1994). Anchoring and grammar effects in judgments of sentence acceptability. *Perceptual and Motor Skills, 79*, 1171-1182.

Ellis, R. (1991). Grammaticality judgments and second language acquisition. *Studies in Second Language Acquisition, 13*, 161-182.

Ferreira, F., & Henderson, J. M. (1991). Recovery from misanalyses of garden-path sentences. *Journal of Memory & Language, 30*(6), 725-745.

Fowler, A. E. (1988). Grammaticality judgments and reading skill in Grade 2. *Annals of Dyslexia, 38*, 73-94.

Frazier, L., & Clifton, C. J. (1996). *Construal*. Cambridge: MIT Press.

Gerken, L., & Bever, T. G. (1986). Linguistic intuitions are the result of interactions between perceptual processes and linguistic universals. *Cognitive Science, 10*, 457-476.

Gescheider, G. A. (1976). *Psychophysics: Method and theory*. Hillsdale, NJ: Lawrence Erlbaum.

Heringer, J. T. (1970). Research on quantifier-negative idiolects. In M. Campbell, J. Lindhohm, A. Davison, W. Fisher, L. Furbee, J. Lovins, E. Maxwell, J. Reighard, & S. Straight (Eds.), *Papers from the sixth regional meeting, Chicago Linguistic Society* (pp. 287-295). Chicago: Chicago Linguistic Society.

Hill, A. A. (1961). Grammaticality. *Word, 17*, 61-73.

Katz, J. J., & Bever, T. G. (1976). The fall and rise of empiricism. In D. T. Langendoen, J. J. Katz, & T. G. Bever (Eds.), *An integrated theory of linguistic ability* (pp. 11-64). New York: Crowell.

Kerlinger, F. N. (1973). *Foundations of behavioral research* (2nd ed.). New York: Holt, Rinehart & Winston.

Kirk, R. E. (Ed.). (1972). *Statistical issues: A reader for the behavioral sciences*. Monterey, CA: Brooks/Cole.

Labov, W. (1972). Some principles of linguistic methodology. *Language in Society, 1*, 97-120.

Labov, W. (1975). Empirical foundations of linguistic theory. In R. P. Austerlitz (Ed.), *The scope of American linguistics: Papers of the first Golden Anniversary Symposium of the Linguistic Society of America, held at the University of Massachusetts, Amherst, on July 24 and 25, 1974* (pp. 77-133). Lisse: Peter de Ridder.

Langendoen, D. T., & Bever, T. G. (1973). Can a not unhappy person be called a not sad one? In S. R. Anderson & P. Kiparsky (Eds.), *A festschrift for Morris Halle*. New York: Holt, Rinehart & Winston.

Linebarger, M. C., Schwartz, M. F., & Saffran, E. M. (1983, December). Syntactic processing in agrammatism: A reply to Zurif and Grodzinsky. *Cognition, 15*(1-3), 215-225.

Lodge, M. (1981). *Magnitude scaling, quantitative measurement of opinions.* Beverly Hills, CA: Sage.

Marks, L. E. (1974). *Sensory processes: The new psychophysics.* New York: Academic Press.

Nagata, H. (1987a). Long-term effect of repetition on judgments of grammaticality. *Perceptual & Motor Skills, 65*(1), 295-299.

Nagata, H. (1987b). Change in the modulus of judgmental scale: An inadequate explanation for the repetition effect in judgments of grammaticality. *Perceptual & Motor Skills, 65*(3), 907-910.

Nagata, H. (1988). The relativity of linguistic intuition: The effect of repetition on grammaticality judgments. *Journal of Psycholinguistic Research, 17*(1), 1-17.

Nagata, H. (1989a). Effect of repetition on grammaticality judgments under objective and subjective self-awareness conditions. *Journal of Psycholinguistic Research, 18*(3), 255-269.

Nagata, H. (1989b). Repetition effect in judgments of grammaticality of sentences: Examination with ungrammatical sentences. *Perceptual & Motor Skills, 68*(1), 275-282.

Nagata, H. (1989c). Judgments of sentence grammaticality and field-dependence of subjects. *Perceptual & Motor Skills, 69*(3, Pt. 1), 739-747.

Nagata, H. (1989d). Judgments of sentence grammaticality with differentiation and enrichment strategies. *Perceptual & Motor Skills, 69*(2), 463-469.

Nagata, H. (1990). Speaker's sensitivity to rule violations in sentences. *Psychologia, 33,* 179-184.

Nagata, H. (1991). On-line judgments of grammaticality of sentences involving rule violations. *Psychologia: An International Journal of Psychology in the Orient, 34*(3), 171-176.

Nagata, H. (1992). Anchoring effects in judging grammaticality of sentences. *Perceptual & Motor Skills, 75*(1), 159-164.

Newmeyer, F. J. (1983). *Grammatical theory.* Chicago: University of Chicago Press.

Popper, K. (1959). *The logic of scientific discovery.* New York: Harper. (Original work published 1935)

Ross, J. R. (1970). On declarative sentences. In R. A. Jacobs & P. S. Rosenbaum (Eds.), *Readings in English transformational grammar* (pp. 222-272). Waltham, MA: Ginn.

Ross, J. R. (1979). Where's English? In C. J. Fillmore, D. Kemper, & W. S. Wang (Eds.), *Individual differences in language ability and language behavior* (pp. 127-163). New York: Academic Press.

Schachter, J., & Yip, V. (1990). Grammaticality judgments: Why does anyone object to subject extraction? *Studies in Second Language Acquisition, 12,* 379-392.

Schütze, C. (1996). *The empirical base of linguistics: Grammaticality judgments and linguistic methodology.* Chicago: University of Chicago Press.

Snow, C., & Meijer, G. (1977). On the secondary nature of syntactic intuitions. In S. Greenbaum (Ed.), *Acceptability in language* (pp. 163-177). The Hague, the Netherlands: Mouton.

Stevens, S. S. (1975). *Psychophysics.* New York: John Wiley.

Stevens, S. S., & Galanter, E. H. (1957). Ratio scales and category scales for a dozen perceptual continua. *Journal of Experimental Psychology, 54*(6), 377-411.

Stokes, W. (1974). All of the work on quantifier-negation isn't convincing. In M. W. La Galy, R. A. Fox, & A. Bruck (Eds.), *Papers from the tenth regional meeting, Chicago Linguistic Society* (pp. 692-700). Chicago: Chicago Linguistic Society.

Wulfeck, B., & Bates, E. (1991). Differential sensitivity to errors of agreement and word order in Broca's aphasia. *Journal of Cognitive Neuroscience, 3*(3), 258-272.

Zribi-Hertz, A. (1989). Anaphor binding and narrative point of view: English reflexive pronouns in sentences and discourse. *Language, 65,* 695-727.

Author Index

Subject Index

Acceptability:
  absolute, 9
  continuous data and, 18, 44, 70
  experiment design for, 39-53
  relative, 22-26
  scaling of, 68-70
  threshold of, 72
  See also Judgments; Stability, of
    judgments
Analysis of variance (ANOVA), 83,
    133-135, 136
  category scale methods and, 120-121
  for informant/token-set data, 122
  significance and, 123, 125
  See also Variance
ANOVA. *See* Analysis of variance
Antecedents, and judgment stability,
    19-22
Arithmetic average. *See* Means
ASCII files, 153
Averages. *See* Means

Benchmark sentences, 92, 117
Between groups variance, 43, 44-45
Binding Theory, and judgment
    stability, 19-22, 139
Blocking, 94, 98-102
  in Excel, 146-152
By-informants summaries, 111, 112-114,
    121-122
By-items summaries. *See* By-materials
    summaries
By-materials summaries, 111-112,
    114-116, 121-122

By-subjects summaries. *See*
    By-informants summaries

Categorical variables, 44
Category scales, 70-72
  data summaries for, 112-114, 115
  response training for, 90
  statistical tests and, 120-121
Central tendency, measures of, 129-130
    See also Means
Coding/decoding, of data, 103-110
  in Excel, 153-157
Cognitive resources, and judgments,
    7-10, 59
Compensation, of informants, 86-87
Competence, compared to
    performance, 7
Computer software:
  for coding/decoding data, 105-109,
    153-157
  for constructing questionnaires, 90,
    96, 143-153
  for presentation modes, 64
  for scanning line drawings, 74-75
  for summarizing data, 158-161
  spreadsheet, 107-110, 112-116
  spreadsheet, Excel, 90, 96, 109,
    117(n3), 141-161
  statistical, 126, 161
  word processor, 106, 110, 152-153
Concatenation function, in Excel, 143
Confidentiality, 87
Context, control of, 51-52
Continuity, of acceptability data, 18, 44, 70

About the Author

Wayne Cowart is Associate Professor of Linguistics at the University of Southern Maine, where he is also Director of the Core Curriculum. He holds a Ph.D. in linguistics from the City University of New York (1983). His research interests include various aspects of the psychology and biology of language and philosophy of mind. His work has appeared in *Language, Memory, and Cognition*, the *Journal of Psycholinguistic Research, Cognition, Perceptual, and Motor Skills*, and various anthologies. Funding for his work has been provided by the National Science Foundation and the National Institutes of Health.